D0430737

Wake, Rise, Resist

Wake, Rise, Resist

The Progressive Teen's Guide to Fighting Tyrants and A*holes

Joanna Spathis & Kerri Kennedy

Contributing Editor:
Jessica Davis

Cover Design by Grace Amandes
www.graceamandes.com

Printed in the United States of America

First Printing, 2017
ISBN-13: 9780999446409 (So's Your Face Press)
ISBN-10: 0999446401

So's Your Face Press
www.sosyourfacepress.com

Visit our website at
www.wakeriseresist.com

For Alejandro, Linus, and Annabeth.
–J.S.

For my Stinker and my Peepers. You are my gift to the future.
–K.K.

And for A.J.

Table of Contents

"This is the upside of the downside."

—GLORIA STEINEM,
WRITER, ACTIVIST, FEMINIST ICON

INTRODUCTION

The Time Is Now

• • •

Dear Reader,

We jokingly started calling this book *We Bet You Think This Book Is About You* as an homage to an old Carly Simon song (look her up on Spotify, young'un) and as a sign of disgust for a certain commander-in-chief's insane ego. But as we have worked on it, we realized that this book—this *time* in our country's history—is about much more than simply resistance to any one person (as loathsome as he may be). It is about the fact that it's time for **action** to push our country forward on its path toward progress. And it's about the fact that *you*— our country's passionate, concerned youth—are exactly who should be leading this march into the future.

We, Joanna and Kerri, are just a couple of regular writers/ editors/neighbors/friends who have been committed to this push for change for about 25 years. (Yeah, your math is correct: we are officially long past being part of the youth culture.) But while we don't share your youth, we do share your feelings of the last year: the horror, the disgust, the desperate wish to affect change.

Friends, we are living in extraordinary times, and it is time for us to become extraordinary ourselves, to stop with our sadness and to get out there, hustle our butts off, and create the loving, accepting, diverse America that has not only equality for all but also justice for all. That change is not coming on its own; it needs us out there, helping to make it happen. To paraphrase a favorite Obama quote: *We* are the change we've been waiting for.

On that horrible Election Night of 2016, a movement to push for change, a *resistance*, was born, and we want you to understand that you, young resistance fighters, are an important part of it—maybe even its most important part. Your country, your world, desperately needs your energy and zeal and passion and optimism and creativity right now.

It's time for us to wake up, rise up, and stand up *together*— ALL of us coming together to create the country and the world that we want. Consider this book your call to action. There *is* indeed a bright future coming, and you are it. Welcome to a new tomorrow.

Onward,
Joanna and Kerri
October 2017

How to Use This Book

What you hold in your hands right now is a guide to try to make the world into the place that we all know it can be ... with some work. This book is a blueprint to that work—filled with lots of actions—tiny ones, big ones, easy ones, hard ones, artsy ones, tech ones ... something (lots of somethings!) for everyone.

It's not a book that you *have* to read in order, but we have set it up in a way that we hope will help you grow into your interests and your activism. We suggest you at least start the book with Chapter 1: You Are Here to help figure out where exactly you want to head in your journey.

From there it's up to you. We suggest you at least skim through the book in order. The first part of the book—I: Building Your Activist Toolkit—is designed to help you assess what you want to do, what you have to work with, and how to set off as an activist.

The second part of the book, Part II: Activism Gets Real, we hope feels more rigorous. We talk candidly about the systemic challenges of our nation and how they prevent us from achieving a fair and healthy society. The section ends with Chapter 6, which launches into the big fights of the day, with *dozens* of ideas, resources, and links to get you started tackling them. (If we say so ourselves, this is the chapter you don't wanna miss.)

Keep reading and you will move on to the final section of the book, Part III: From Activist to Advocate. There you will find how to inspire others, raise awareness, and live your life with the intention and effectiveness of a true advocate.

What we have created is a way for you to get started early on your commitment to progress. *You* will shape the future—and you are starting this very day. Hurry, please. Your movement needs you.

1. What do you bring to the table?

What's the common factor in all of the actions in this book? You!

Everyone, regardless of their age or where they live, has something valuable to contribute. You might not even recognize the kinds of gifts you will bring to the movement. You may have specific personal skills, such as the ability to imagine yourself in someone else's shoes or the gift of connecting with people easily. You may have certain character traits, such as a certain infectious optimism, a passionate enthusiasm, or a healthy skepticism. Whatever your talents, big, small, or cheeky, you bring with you a voice, an accumulation of experiences, and a youthful capacity to picture a healthier world.

For your first action, explore all of the talents and skills that make you *you*. Make a list of all the qualities you can offer. We mean everything from your singing voice, jump shot, and baking skills to your ability to stay cool when others run hot. What are you good at? (Like, for example, are you good at motivating others? Or maybe you're good with a deadline or you're good at thinking creatively?) What do you and don't you enjoy? (Maybe you enjoy writing or enjoy being physically active or don't enjoy meeting lots of new people at once but are great with small groups.) What excites you? (You might be excited about working as part of a team, for example, or you might be excited about helping to spread a message.) Keep your list handy to help guide you in your activism.

PART ONE

BUILDING YOUR ACTIVIST TOOLKIT

• • •

"You cannot, you cannot use someone else's fire.
You can only use your own.
And in order to do that,
you must first be willing to
believe that you have it."

—AUDRE LORDE,
POET AND ACTIVIST

CHAPTER ONE

You Are Here

Actions to Start Your Journey of Activism

• • •

"Sometimes it falls upon a generation to
be great. You can be that generation."

—NELSON MANDELA,
ACTIVIST AND SOUTH AFRICAN PRESIDENT

Friend,

You came of age with eloquence at the helm. President
Barack Obama, now there's a guy who could speak and feel
and think and lead. I wish we could linger here a few pages,
but the truth is we are not in Obama's America anymore.
I don't know how he did it. I don't even think *he* really
knows how he did, but Donald Trump is in office now and
there's no sugarcoating it: the sh*t just got real—real fast!

I know you want to jump into the resistance, push back hard,
march, maybe scream and scream some more. Believe me, you

are not alone. But if you can hold off and keep your wonderful wits about you, this is the chapter that lines up your ducks and sets you on course. It's like vitamins or tuning your guitar. No, it's like flossing! It's not necessarily the funnest stuff, but it's the prep that lays the foundation for a future of activism. The activism this country needs. Activism with a strong, clean bite.

Let's do this!
Joanna

2. What's your issue? Make a list!

Make a list of the issues you care about: what you're worried about, what you wish were different, what you want to protect. (Feeling lost? Turn to the Passion Index at the back of the book to help you out with some topic ideas.) Put your list online on a Pinterest board, if you wish, or keep it private in the notes app on your phone or just on a piece of paper. The list may include personal and family concerns—issues related to your community, to your faith, to your future—as well as injustices outside of your personal experience that grab your attention and won't let go.

Let your list grow and change in the days and weeks and months ahead. It'll probably be long. And maybe overwhelming. (Don't worry: you don't have to work on everything—this is just a brainstorming exercise.) Invite others to add their own notes and ideas. Start scanning your neighborhood, reading newspapers, listening to what other people care about and add them to your own ideas. Let this list be the roadmap of where you want to head (and then let it serve as a reminder to keep you moving in that direction).

As your list grows, add new ideas, new worries, new goals, and new notes as you start to become more conscious of the issues around you. If there's a particular issue or cause that feels especially important to you, circle it or highlight it or add 10 exclamation points!!!!!!!!!! (See how legit that looks?) You may want to stick the list to a wall where you can see it regularly to remind you of your ideas. (You may need a poster board. Heck, you may need a bigger wall!)

3. Before you go bold or go anywhere ... schedule a meeting

Now would be a good time to talk to your family about your activism. Make an actual invitation: write down a time and place (like after Tuesday dinner or before Sunday breakfast). Use the invitation to explain to your family what is important to you. Include a loose agenda so that whoever is invited can think about the things you want to discuss before the meeting. Talk to them about getting involved. What are your concerns? Their concerns? Are there any boundaries they'd like you to uphold?

Depending on where you live, certain actions might make you feel or be vulnerable. Discuss that as a team. Will you speak up for others who are vulnerable (if you aren't vulnerable at the time)? What role will social media play in your activism? Are you on the same page with your adults as far as the rules and expectations for both real life and for social media and email contacts?

This is a good time to think about and gather input about what kind of activist you imagine yourself being and what kind of activism your family pictures for you. Maybe you want to push back, march, make your voice heard? Maybe you're more comfortable supporting a cause that has lost some of its funding or has moved out of the spotlight. Make a family date to meet again for further discussion once you get your feet wet as an activist.

It sounds a little formal but it's a good idea to take notes during the meeting about what is discussed—the ideas, the concerns, any rules laid down, etc. Then email them to everyone involved so they can review the notes. This way, everyone is totally on the same page about what was discussed and decided. This prevents misunderstandings and keeps parents' faulty memories from misremembering what happened.

Listen Up

Fair warning: sometimes tempers can get heated when politics are involved or family is involved. When politics *and* families are involved, well, things could get tense. Set up some ground rules to ensure that everyone has time to speak and everyone has time to listen. You can use a prop, for example, and only the person holding the prop can talk at that point. Go into the meeting understanding that your family might have some concerns, and be ready to hear and address those concerns. Showing a willingness to compromise validates everyone's perspective and goes a long way toward neutralizing tension.

4. What are you working with?

You may live in a community of like-minded family and friends, where there are many people working toward many of the same things. Know that you are lucky! You may feel lonely where you live, like there aren't many people or organizations that believe in the same things you do. Know that you can still work actively to make a difference!

Either way, assess what you have going for you. What are you working with in your area? Write down a list of your resources. Do you have computer access? Do you have permission to post to social media? Is there a local paper? Do you know who is in your local government and how it is run? Who is on your school board? Do you have a trusted teacher? A like-minded sister? Is there a local organization that is politically active? What other local organizations are there around that might share your values or goals? Think about who's in your corner and what kinds of things, places, or people could be helpful to you. Put your list somewhere safe for you to consult when you're in action mode. Here's hoping that your list grows as you become more involved!

5. Check out your library

The public library can be the activist's best friend. It often has computers, printers, and copiers to help for completing projects. Your library might also have free meeting spaces available to you for planning sessions for projects. Probably most important: the library has librarians, who are often perfect resources for information about the world at large and about your community.

Go to your local public library (if you're lucky enough to have one nearby), and get to know it. Explore its events calendar and its website and see what it has to offer. While you're there, befriend a librarian and explain your goals. They are great for recommendations and for directing you toward information. (Yes, fellow grammar geeks, we're using *they* instead of *he* or *she* because it's lovingly gender-expansive, rather than binary. Sometimes you have to bend rules for the greater good. But give yourself 2 points for noticing.)

May We Suggest ...

Don't have a local library or are not getting the help that you need with a question you have? Did you know that the New York Public Library Reference desk has taken questions via telephone since 1968? (They got so many great questions, in fact, that they published a reference book with the questions and answers.) AskNYPL still takes calls, and you can now also text, email, chat, or Tweet (@ AskNYPL) a question. The service is open to everyone, and no question is too strange. (For proof, check out the AskNYPL Instagram feed for posts of some of their all-time-favorite questions.)

6. Become civic-minded

It's easier to become more politically active when you understand a little something about the way that the government operates. Sure you've studied it in school, but everyone needs a little refresher now and again. Outside of cracking open a textbook, there are lots of ways to remind yourself about the civics of how our country operates and why it works that way:

- Start off at the National Constitution Center (constitutioncenter.org), a nonpartisan group that dedicates itself to teaching about the Constitution; check out the Learn tab to see what it offers and listen to its "We the People" podcast to learn even more.
- While you're listening to podcasts, also check out Radio Lab Presents: More Perfect (www.wnyc.org/shows/radiolabmoreperfect)—which is Radio Lab's look at important Supreme Court cases.
- Look at TED-Ed's YouTube channel. Search the channel for "civics," and you will find lots of easy-to-understand videos explaining different parts of the democratic process.
- Test all of your knowledge with the games at iCivics (www.icivics.org), which was started by Justice Sandra Day O'Connor back in 2009.

7. Know who represents you

You can picture political representation as a series of ever-smaller circles, such as those on a target. The biggest circle is the national level (those are the folks in Washington, D.C.). Then the next-smallest ring is the state level, smaller still is the county level, and the smallest is the city/town level. (You could even make an argument that your school student council is an even-smaller ring still.)

Before you do any actions, find out who represents you. Go to Contacting Congress (contactingcongress.org) to look up the names and info for your two senators and your congressperson (each area of a state has one person in the House of Representatives to represent it). Follow them on social media, and upload or cut and paste their contact info (address and phone numbers—there will be several listed so write them all down) as well as their political parties. Keep the info handy because you will likely be checking it a lot!

Also look up your state governor and state representatives. (Go to usa.gov/elected-officials to look up your state politicians as well as possibly your county and local-level politicians, if your area is populated enough.)

Go the Extra Step

Politicians and candidates publish position papers that show their stances on different topics. These can usually be found on their websites. If you don't know much about who represents you, read up on their positions. Interested in learning even more? Go to www.govtrack.us/congress/ votes to see their voting record.

8. This is your mission ... choose to accept it

Go forward throughout the rest of this book with intention. Whether you call it a sense of purpose, an intention, or a mission, we all need some kind of goal to be effective. Most of us get through our day moving from one activity or obligation to another—having some fun when we can and working hard when we should. But if you were told that this week your mission was to learn to play the ukulele, would you live your days any differently? Would having a defined purpose, an *intention*, change some of the choices in your day? This is the power of a mission statement—it's a thoughtful definition of your intention, one that factors in your values, your expectations, and your dreams. And while most people live without such a statement of intention, you might be amazed to see how helpful they can be.

Sit down and write a mission statement for your activism. The statements should be general and generous (see an example below); you don't want to confine yourself or pen yourself in; it should instead help guide you and inform your decision-making. Write one with your family as well. A family mission statement puts you on the same page and is a terrific launching point for making decisions as a group.

May We Suggest ...

If you feel like you need more guidance, here is Joanna's personal mission statement as a model:

It is my mission: To use my talents and skills for a greater good; To seize every opportunity to learn new things, reach out to new people, and imagine even the unimaginable; To define what I believe to be important based on my most generous values; To recognize that I am powerful enough right now, as is, and that I deserve the life that I want for myself and everyone else.

9. Sign of your times

You have spent this section learning more about yourself and the community around you. You have gathered information about your beliefs, your family's beliefs, and your community's beliefs and have set a mission for yourself to guide your journey of activism. Before you move on to the next section, create something to remind yourself of your intentions. How 'bout a sign? It should convey a message that's important to you—one that reminds you of your mission statement. It also lets others know that you take a stand for what you believe. It could be a simple peace sign, an inspiring quote, or a declaration to a cause. Keep it positive, and make it inspiring.

Sadly, it's important to remember that even in the most seemingly progressive communities, hate and bigotry exist. In these tension-filled times even simple declarations of kindness are under attack. Cowards steal and vandalize signs every day, everywhere. If you can imagine being targeted for your beliefs, keep yourself safe: put your symbol of intention somewhere like your bedroom wall rather than in your window.

CHAPTER TWO

Building on a Common Ground

Actions to Expand Your Bubble

● ● ●

"I know there is strength in the
differences between us.
I know there is comfort, where we overlap."

—ANI DiFRANCO,
SINGER-SONGWRITER

Dear Reader,

For me, love has always been front and center of why I believe what I do. My love for other human beings, my love for my earth and the wondrous beauty in it, and my love for justice and fairness. (Hey, I'm a youngest child—we are *all* about what is and isn't fair!) After the election, it felt like my belief system had shattered into a trillion pieces. How could so many people elect someone who so clearly did not stand for any of the things that I believed in so passionately?

Now I see how privileged I was to have lived so snuggly in that shiny, happy bubble for so long. I thought my beliefs had shattered that Election Night. They hadn't. I still have them (and still believe in them passionately). What had shattered was my wrong-headed, bubbled-off understanding that the world was automatically tilting toward what is good and right and that I didn't need to be in the fight to make that happen.

We can no longer lie to ourselves that being passive in our beliefs is an option: we must become active warriors for what is good and right and just. (Superhero cape optional.) And the first step in doing so is to burst our bubbles (or at least nudge them a little bigger with our elbows). We must recognize that there's a world outside of our safe spaces and that we must honestly see that world for what it's like and not just what we want it to be. That's what this chapter is for—to help us grow out of our comfort zones and learn to see the world how it really is. The work is hard … but worth it. With your new understanding will come respect, compassion, appreciation, and, yes, even a renewed love for the beautiful diversity that is this country and this world.

Ever from a place of love,
Kerri

10. Spread empathy

Empathy is what helps us understand where other people are coming from—what their life is like and what it would be like to live that life. Empathy is what helps a person who lives in urban Washington, D.C., be able to picture what life is like for someone in rural Nebraska (and vice versa). It's what helps an American picture the life of a Syrian. And it's what is all too lacking in some people who can't see past their own privilege to understand the realities of others (see below for more on privilege).

When you hear a friend saying something unempathetic—maybe saying that all homeless people are just greedy and want money for nothing—then try to spread empathy: Remind your friend that homeless people are sisters and brothers to someone and that they aren't living some great, comfy life coasting off others. Help your friend picture a day and a night in the life of a homeless person, and see if you can plant a seed to grow some more empathy in this world.

11. P is for privilege

Chances are if you haven't thought much about privilege, you have loads of it. Privilege—an unearned advantage, right, or protection given to an individual or group—is a complicated issue that has finally taken its rightful place in the national discussion. The first step in understanding privilege is to examine your own. Begin by thinking about your advantages and disadvantages and how they make up your *vantage point*, the position from which you see. Picture this scenario: You're an able-bodied person crossing the street and come to a high curb. Chances are, you don't have to visualize raising your leg and stepping up on that curb. Your vantage point as able-bodied is to not give curbs a second thought: you just step and go.

Now imagine the curb from the vantage point of someone who uses a wheelchair. Suddenly that curb puts you at a disadvantage, right? If you're in a wheelchair, you've had to think about curbs *a lot*. Now imagine you wheel into a city council meeting to talk about adding ramps to the curbs. The council members who make the decisions are *all* able-bodied people with able-bodied vantage points. You make your request for ramps, and one of them says, "I have no problem with the curbs. In fact, no one on this city council has ever had problems with the curbs."

Is it absurd for able-bodied people to make decisions without considering other vantage points? Yep! And also privileged. People who have privilege say and do absurd things all. the. time. And the *really* crummy part is they are so blind to their privilege they often don't even know they're being absurd. But the time has come (more than come!) for those who have privilege to start seeing it and start learning to understand other, non-privileged viewpoints.

Once you recognize privilege, you'll begin to really "see" it in all its absurdity. Like how privileged voter ID laws are because not everyone can afford to take time off work to get an ID and not everyone can afford even a modest fee to pay for one. Or how privileged male politicians feel to make health care decisions about what is and is not medically necessary for women.

Why do so many people refuse to recognize their privilege? Quite frankly, it's hard work—and it requires humility and self awareness. And even once people know to see their privilege, they will first feel pretty uncomfortable and defensive about it. But push past those instincts of defensiveness or discomfort, and you will be rewarded with a more honest view of society and who has what and why. This is not a pretty reality, but it is an authentic one. Only once we can see privilege can we start working to slowly undo its powerful and ugly legacy.

12. Be a citizen and student of the world

Americans have a bad rap for not knowing much about the rest of the world. You can be more worldly than that! Pick a country and research it online. Where is it? What are its people like? What do they eat, speak, study? What is this country's history? Is it an established country, or is there still a lot of unrest? How are people treated? Use Google Earth to see what it looks like in different areas of the country. Does it make you want to visit? See if you can find an English-language newspaper from the area and read up on its local news and also how it interprets the news coming from the United States. Look for an authentic local recipe online, and get a taste of the local culture.

13. Eat the world

People have immigrated to this country from every corner of the world. You'd be surprised that even in smaller American towns you will find people from seemingly everywhere. If you live in or near even a small city, you'll probably be able to find a restaurant that features the proud cuisine of a different culture than you're used to. Approach the experience with a generous, open mind. Be willing to taste new things. Show respectful curiosity about the menu. For example, ask why a particular food is treasured in the culture. It may feel like just lunch, but it sends a message to the shop owner that you are open and welcoming. Thank them for the chance to get a taste of a different part of the world.

If you can't take a drive to, say, an Ethiopian restaurant, you could still learn something (delicious) by trying a recipe for *injera*, an Ethiopian flat bread on which the cuisine's many tasty stews are served. Encourage your family to eat the bread traditionally: from a communal platter, with each person tearing off a piece of bread to scoop up whatever you've placed on top of it. Food and culture often go hand in hand, so savor not just the cuisine, but the chance to learn more about the area that it comes from.

14. Learn another language

The world has lots of beautiful, wonderful cultures within it, and one of the greatest things about our country is how so many of those cultures are also represented within our boundaries. When we study another language, we get a glimpse into the lives of another culture and we grow an appreciation for other parts of the world. And lucky for us modern folk that learning a language has never been easier. Free languages classes are all over the Internet—including some great ones on YouTube.

Plus if you study long enough and hard enough, you'll be able to talk with members of that culture in their own language. They'll appreciate your efforts, and you may learn a lot more in the process than you would if you had been trying to converse in English.

15. Read your way to a better understanding

There are lots of places in this country where diversity is just a fantasy—where most neighbors have the same racial or cultural background. Given this reality, sometimes it can be frustrating to try to better understand other worldviews when you can't see other types of people right in front of you each day. Books to the rescue!

To get you started on finding good-quality reads to help you see another viewpoint, turn to either your librarian friend from Action #5 (librarians rock!) or to some high-quality lists on the Internet:

- Check out the Coretta Scott King Award winners (www. ala.org/emiert/cskbookawards).

- The Jane Addams Children's Book Awardees (www. janeaddamspeace.org/jacba) are great even for teens and adults.
- The Arab American Book Award Winners (www. arabamericanmuseum.org/bookaward) has categories for fiction, nonfiction, poetry, and children/young adult.
- Check out the Book Dragon: Books for the MultiCulti Reader (smithsonianapa.org/bookdragon) blog, which is created by the Smithsonian Asian Pacific American Center and includes books for all ages.

May We Suggest ...
Too busy to read a whole book? Try finding the audiobook and carve out some time to listen. (Check to see if your library offers access to free audiobooks through your phone or device.)

16. Listen your way to a better understanding

Of course, not every culture and group is well represented by traditional books. Many oppressed peoples simply have not had—and still do not have—easy access to publication. Finding these viewpoints and traditions can be more difficult and are usually most widely accessible through alternative "languages" such as music, dance, fashion, and food.

Oral storytelling is also often part of these cultures and can offer more insight into these all-too-easily-hidden groups. Groundswell: Oral History for Social Change (www.oralhistoryforsocialchange. org) is *holy smokes!* amazing and includes links to oral history projects in its Resources section. Check out the Mixtape project (in the Projects area) to find links to work like the Winnemem Wintu Oral History Project and the American Jewish Peace Archive. Be sure to also check out the Archives section for more links. Load up your playlist, and learn more about the vast types of people in the world around us.

17. Join the club

If you're lucky, your school already has a club for the LGBTQ community. If you are LGBTQ and aren't already a member, become one! (If you aren't LGBTQ, check first to be sure the club is open to cisfriends and then—when you go—honor the fact that this is a safe space for others. Safe spaces are where members of a group can speak freely without worrying about the feelings, thoughts, or judgments of someone outside the group.) Whatever your orientation, join the club as an act of showing that you want safe spaces for all people in your school and because you believe that diversity is an opportunity and not a limitation.

If your school does not have any such club, join up with some friends and a staff member and start one. The Genders & Sexualities Alliance Network (gsanetwork.org) offers thorough advice on starting a group. Go to Get Involved and then Start a GSA to find a lot of helpful, concrete information.

18. Work toward being an ally

OK, so imagine you are a non-Muslim who is sick to your stomach about how Muslims have been treated, and you just discovered there is a Muslim advocacy group that meets nearby. *That's great!* Now just may be a good time to join that group in solidarity. *And perhaps it is!* But before you run into a meeting ready to profess that you're an ally to Muslims and here to help ... [cue screeching brakes sound] ... *STOP.* Let's talk about what it means to be an ally.

Here's the bottom line: friends and allies are two different things. You get to call yourself a friend, but only someone inside a community can call you an ally. To try to become worthy of being called an ally, you're gonna need to do some work. For example, you might read some articles about Muslim advocacy written by *Muslim* activists. Then go to your first three, five, ten meetings with your eyes open and your mouth shut (because—um, no—despite what teachers may tell you, a bit of homework does *not* really make you an expert). Let yourself listen—truly listen—to the real experts at these meetings: listen to learn, listen to honor, and listen to respect. Ask a member of the group privately after a meeting if, how, and when the group can use your support. Actively listen to what they need. Be willing to work hard in your supporting (*not* starring) role in the group.

Work to live your life by these principles as well—in trying to be an ally to others unlike yourself, go in with a growth mindset (see Action #55) and know that you are not—and never will be—the expert on what this group needs, wants, or should do. Keep doing your homework, keep learning from others about their realities and their challenges, and keep listening to the truths that those inside the fight are telling you. Allies are needed in the struggle for justice, no doubt. But allies are made, not declared.

19. Discover pop culture of another culture

Popular culture of any region or of any group becomes popular for a reason—because it reflects some piece of the people it represents. (Not to mention that it's usually hugely catchy.) By looking into what's popular in someone else's culture or region, we get a little insight into that part of them. (Plus it gives us something interesting and specific to talk about with people we meet who are from other places or whose backgrounds are not like our own.)

It is now easier than ever to access music from other cultures and learn about different viewpoints that way. Diversify your playlist (and worldview) by checking out the latest from another part of the world or just another part of our country. You may live far from rural areas and have no idea how much you'd like country music. Maybe you're already a big country music fan? Listen to rap ... or salsa ... or bluegrass ... or blues ... or K-pop ... or ranchera music ... or, well, you get the idea. Also see if you can find any videos for the music on YouTube to get an even deeper insight into the culture it represents. Make this action into a fun challenge by setting a goal to listen to at least two songs from every continent in the next month. (Good luck with Antarctica!)

Go the Extra Step

When you start looking at the music of another culture, keep in mind that it's possible that the more popular stuff might be highly Americanized (the Americanization of world culture is all too real). Dig down in your searches to find the indie singers and groups—those who care less about their images or their brands and those who care more about the message that they are sending out. Often these musicians aren't just entertainers, they are the thinkers, activists, educators, historians, and changemakers of their generation.

20. Visit a museum ... in your pajamas

While we wish that we had money to help each of you travel this wonderful country of ours to learn about our wonderful diversity, we are sad to report no such funds exist. But never fear! You can still roam the country to learn about other cultures—you just have to do the traveling online. Take a break from aimlessly watching Netflix or checking out yet another YouTube prank video and instead devote some of your online time to checking out the digital displays at a museum that celebrates the various cultures and ethnicities that make up the American people. (There are, of course, a LOT of other wonderful museums and digital exhibits out there. This is just a list to get you started on your expeditions. Safe digital travels, young resistance member.)

- The National Museum of African American History & Culture (in Washington, D.C.) offers loads of online exhibitions (check out the Explore section): nmaahc.si.edu
- America's Islamic Heritage Museum & Cultural Center (in Washington, D.C.) has online exhibits as well as a YouTube channel and active social media feeds: www.aihmuseum. org/scholars--corner.html
- Arab American National Museum (in Dearborn, Michigan) links to many permanent online exhibits through its Library & Resources section: www.arabamericanmuseum.org
- Smithsonian Asian Pacific American Center (in Washington, D.C. with several traveling exhibits all over the country) features digital exhibits as well as active blogs: smithsonianapa.org

Go the Extra Step

After your virtual visit, go to the Contact link and send a letter of support to the museum staff thanking them for helping the various cultures of America to come to life for even online visitors. (Ask permission before you email or give out contact information.)

21. Be a book scout

There are many, many, many wonderful children's and young adult books that can help you see other cultures and learn about their realities and lives. You're going to have to do a little recon for this action. Your mission? To find lots of those kinds of books at your local library (thank goodness for that librarian friend you made in Action #5). The second part of this mission is to help others find the books, too: put a sticky note flagging up from their covers with info on why people should read them. For example, you might sticky *Inside Out and Back Again* (by Thanhha Lai) with a note saying, "This book taught me so much about how scary it is to have your home lost to a war and to have to start over in a new country. It helped me see what it's like to be forced to become a refugee." (Snap a pic of your sticky note on the book, and post it online!)

22. Reach out to an immigrant or a culture

The anti-immigrant trolls are out in full, ugly force. Do you know people who've recently immigrated to this country? Send them a postcard and say thanks for coming to make our country more diverse and beautiful and express your support for keeping the country open to immigrants such as them.

You could also send a postcard to any cultural group that's come under fire—such as sending a postcard of appreciation to a mosque—and let them know you're happy they're here. These are little gestures, it's true, but these little gestures can make the difference between feeling alienated and feeling supported. Reach out.

Go the Extra Step

Are there immigrant students in your school? Talk to the ESL (English as a Second Language) teacher about getting involved in ESL tutoring or identify yourself as a peer resource for an immigrant student who might need support acclimating to a new country.

23. Find a pen pal

It's not like you can just write a letter to a refugee to learn more about what life is like for her ... or can you? Some organizations match up pen pals between students and young refugees living in camps overseas, but you have to sign up as a group to take part. Ask your English teacher or service club sponsor if your class/group can sign up. (If that doesn't work out, find a teacher to sponsor a new global club and meet after school to write refugees.)

The Canadian organization RESPECT (respectrefugees.org) is one place that organizes a global letter exchange program. Sign up and help yourself and your class learn more about the harsh realities of refugee life and the less-harsh realities that refugees are really just people, too. You might be surprised how much you have in common.

24. Interview a vet

It's hard to understand what members of the military have gone through if you've never been in the armed forces. Talking with a vet is the perfect way to open your eyes to the real problems and struggles of people who have served this country. No matter how you might feel about war or the military, it is important to remember that these are still people with critical needs who are often slipping through the cracks and being left behind.

If you have the opportunity to interview someone who has served in the military, seize it! Be sure to spend some time researching the conflict and its history before the interview. Come prepared with thoughtful questions. Before the interview, ask the veteran if there is anything she would rather not talk about: some topics are sensitive. If it's okay with her, ask not only about her time in the military but also about her time after the military or after deployment—how she was treated and felt after returning home. It can be enlightening to learn about the physical and mental health care struggles that veterans often face after serving and can be a reminder on why keeping veteran affairs at the forefront of politics is important.

The Library of Congress Veterans History Project (www.loc.gov/vets) features oral-history interviews with veterans of wars starting with World War I and includes participants of modern wars such as Afghanistan. Ask your interviewee if you may submit your audio to the project.

25. Think about cultural appropriation

We wish we had space to fully explain the nuanced and layered topic of cultural appropriation, but the truth is it's a subject you kind of have to dive in and swim around before you can even begin to grasp it. What we do have space enough to do is to advise you to learn about what is cultural appreciation and what is cultural *appropriation* and about the important differences between the two. Cultural appreciation is when someone from one culture works to understand and respect the honored traditions of another culture. Cultural appropriation is when one group adopts the cultural markers of an oppressed group; that dominant group takes something with deep meaning and reduces it to mere toys or fashion. (Think: white people wearing cornrows or non-indigenous people dressing up as Pocahontas or wearing headdresses for fashion).

We advise you to dive in and learn more about cultural appropriation. It's not an easy subject. Author and media critic K. Tempest Bradford has built an outstanding series of essays designed to teach about cultural appropriation. You can find the series at Medium (medium.com). Search "Cultural Appropriation Primer" (or go to https://medium.com/@tempest/the-cultural-appropriation-primer-91f1101dae1d).

26. Travel when you can

Many people grow up never leaving their small section of the world. Sometimes that's not a choice, but sometimes it is. Aspire to travel!

Travel offers a rich opportunity to see what other countries are like—besides being hella interesting. Grow your curiosity, wander any part of the world that you can, seize every opportunity. Travel grows your understanding that people in other cultures aren't some scary "other" people but are—much like Americans—simply doing what they can to live full, happy lives.

If world travel isn't a realistic option for you anytime soon, spend some time cultivating a wanderlust spirit. Even if you don't make it off your front porch, you will benefit from growing your sense of adventure and sense of the global culture.

27. Smell fear

You've now spent a whole section practicing seeing the world beyond your backyard, beyond the person you see in the mirror or those you see at the lunchroom table. It's a section about celebrating the gorgeous diversity of our country and using that diversity and multiculturality to make the movement stronger.

Before you leave this section, take a few minutes to think about how fear (or avoiding fear!) is a super-powerful motivator, and—since we all have our own fears of *something*—it's one that everyone can relate to. Fear is a cheap, easy way to keep people mindlessly following along behind you. If children learn (or are taught outright) to fear certain people or things to keep them "safe," then an authoritarian leader (*ahem*) could use those same fears to get people to accept sacrifices to civil liberties and call it safety. It's a disgusting cycle. Fear is created; fear is fed to gain power; fear grows; even more power is gained.

Companies, groups, and leaders manipulate people all the time through fear: "Afraid your friends will say you smell bad? Well, we've got the deodorant for you!" Sounds familiar, right? How different is that than, say: "Afraid a transgendered person is really only a predator in the bathroom? Let's pass a law preventing them from using the bathroom they want." (Never mind that it's utterly ridiculous to equate transgendered people with predators. These manipulators are using the fear to get to what they want—exclusion and dominance.)

Being aware of how you are being manipulated by fear is powerful—like a superhero kind of powerful! So the next time someone tells you that all Muslims are extremists and want to hurt all Americans, smell the fear this person is trying to grow. Tell him or her what you know to be true: that Islam is a peaceful, loving religion and billions of Muslims are as happily and lovingly living their lives as Christians and Jews and atheists and Sikhs and all of the other wonderful belief systems of this world. If you are in a space where it feels safe to do so, tell people like this that they are being manipulated to fear what or who they do not know. (If you don't feel safe, then remove yourself from the situation and get yourself somewhere safe pronto.)

CHAPTER THREE

Craft Your Message

Actions to Find What You Want to Say

• • •

"No one can make us feel invisible
when we demand to be seen."

—AMANDA NYUGEN,

ACTIVIST

Friend,

Roughly a zillion years ago a writer once told me, "If it comes from your heart, it will be beautiful." Truthfully, that isn't the kind of line that motivates me. It's nonsense, right? How do they know it'll be beautiful? I've certainly written my share of less-than-beautiful words. But for roughly a zillion years now I've been thinking about that line, shaking my head, poking holes at its reasoning. I hate the line. But time and time again, when I'm feeling insecure, when I'm wondering how to write something, say something, approach something, I say it to myself. *If it comes from my heart, it will be beautiful.*

This chapter is about helping you find and hone and use your voice as an activist. And I'll say this to you: *If it comes from your heart, friend, it will be beautiful.* I'm not going to defend the phrasing, but I will urge you to go ahead and internalize it. Spend a couple decades poking holes at it, dismissing it ... but trust it nonetheless. Your voice, the way you see the world, your perspective, what you think is important, it's not all going to be gold, but it'll be YOURS. Your authentic, compassionate, earnest voice is beautiful. It just is. I don't know how it works. You don't have to believe me, just see for yourself.

We're all ears!
Joanna

28. Check your sources ... twice

If the 2016 election taught us anything, it's how vulnerable the Internet is to crummy, false information (and how vulnerable we humans are to believing it). Before you set out to share your message, be sure any facts that you are using are actual, honest-to-goodness facts. Check your sources at PolitiFact (politifact.com), FactCheck.org (factcheck. org), or Snopes (snopes.com). Better yet, check all *three* places if you have time.

Beyond that, also think critically about where you get your information. Don't believe everything you see on Instagram or other social media. (Heck, don't even believe everything you read on most websites!) Even if you're looking at a reputable news source, look carefully at the page. Is it labeled "Opinion," "Editorial," "Perspective," or "Analysis" somewhere near the article title? If so, it is not necessarily a news story—it's the opinion of the writer. Or does it have a line anywhere about being "Sponsored Content"? If so, it's been paid for by someone and only made to *look* like a real news story. (As advertising money has gotten harder to get, some sources have started offering sponsored content or native advertising—things designed to look like real, reputable news articles—to boost their incomes.)

Whatever you are reading, whatever you are using to get info, use a healthy suspicion to develop your critical eye. Does this sound like opinion to you, or does it sound like news? Does it sound like all voices are being included (news sources historically are pretty crummy about including voices of oppressed peoples). If something sounds at all fishy, check it out and then pass along only the good info. We'll all be the wiser for it.

29. Go back in time

Learn the backstory on a topic you're interested in. You might study the history of refugees in this country, for example. (Sure, you could research online at a reputable source such as the awesome Zinn Education Project at zinnedproject.org, but remember that friendly librarian you got to know in Action #5? Ask him or her for some books to help you on your research.) A quick tip: look at children's nonfiction books. It sounds crazy, but those short, easy-to-understand books cover big topics in a quick, easy-to-digest way. If you have time for a long adult book, by all means, go for it. But if you need something you can scan through quickly, the children's section is the place to be. Whatever you decide to read, keep in mind that not all perspectives and cultures are well represented in written history.

Looking at even a small slice of history can really give insight into the trends and cycles of the topic. For example, the U.S. attitude toward accepting refugees has changed dramatically over the course of our nation's history. (Look at, say, how Jewish refugees were treated before, during, and after World War II, or look at how early Irish immigrants were treated compared to later in history.) Once you've done some research, sit down and try to picture the broad arc of history for this subject. And think about what's happening today—say, the current refugee crisis and the American response to it? Are we doing enough? (See Action #68 for more information on working for refugees and immigrants.)

30. Specialize yourself

It might feel like the earth is shifting under your feet when you see all that is under attack right now. So zero in on a few things you care about—education, the environment, gun control, Islamophobia, whatever!—and focus yourself like a laser on those one or two topics. It's better to focus on an issue (or two) rather than taking on the whole world. Make it your *thing*. Study it, learn about it, and take a look at the people and groups already fighting for it and what they're doing....

Once you've chosen your focus, look around for a way to get involved (Chapter 6 will help, too!). There are many reputable groups for just about any topic that you decide to take on, and groups such as Movement Match (jointhemovementtoday.weebly. com) and Activism Engine (activismengine.org) are working to connect activists to groups that need their passion. Stay Woke's Resistance Manual also has lists and lists (and lists!) of ways to get involved: www.resistancemanual.org/Organizations_Working_for_Justice_and_Equity (or go to www.resistancemanual.org and scroll down to Resource Pages).

May We Suggest ...
We have a list of our activities broken up by what we call a "passion index" at the back of the book. See what inspires you to get involved. Good luck!

31. Study your role models
This is an easy action because it's all about the good: Yay for positivity! All you need to do is look around for the good in your world and then

try to see who is helping to make that good happen. Identify those people who are acting the way you would want to act and doing what you would want to do, and make them your role models. It might be a family member or a coach or a local activist. Or it might even be someone you read about online or see in the news.

If possible, try to interview your role model (or role models—it's great to have more than one). If it's someone you already know, that's perfect: just reach out and say that you like what they've been doing and ask if you can talk to them about how they go about it. If it's not someone you know, then write an email asking them for some advice.

May We Suggest ...
Looking for a role model? The world is full of 'em! May we suggest that you read up on these amazing young people?

- Amanda Nyugen, activist for the civil rights of survivors of sexual assault and rape: @nguyen_amanda
- Christopher Yao, youth activist who founded Kids Change the World (kidschangetheworld.org), which organizes youth to work on global education and health
- Cierra Fields, indigenous student activist fighting to raise the age of consent from 14 to 16: @CierraFields918
- Cristina Jiménez, executive director and cofounder of United We Dream, an immigrant youth-led advocacy organization: @CrisAlexJimenez

- Darius Weems, disability rights activist and fundraiser who died in October 2016; his ability to inspire continues: @DariusGoesWest
- Gavin Grimm, transgender student who took his right to use the boys bathroom at school to court: @GavinGrimmVA
- Hebh Jamal, student activist fighting Islamophobia and the immigration ban: @hebh_jamal
- Johnetta Elzie, civil rights activist and leader in the group We the Protestors: @_Nettaaaaaaaaa
- Lizzie Velásquez, disability rights activist and YouTuber who works to end bullying: @littlelizziev
- Lydia X. Z. Brown, autism and disability rights activist also focusing on intersectionality and intersectional social justice: @autistichoya
- Tegan and Sara, rock band formed by twin sisters, both lesbians and outspoken LGBTQ activists: @teganandsara
- Xiuhtezcatl Martinez, climate change activist and youth director of Earth Guardians conservation organization: @XiuhtezcatlM

32. Who's Repre$enting you?

Want to better understand politics? Unfortunately, that often means you have to follow the money. It's a murky, murky question about a murky, murky part of our political world, but it's important, and you should have a working understanding of it. Action

#71 dives deeper into these sinister waters, but there are a couple of basic things you should know off the bat.

First things first, money is <u>everywhere</u> in politics. We may elect our representatives, but all too often, our representatives are *representing* other people, groups, corporations, and whole industries who pay lots and lots of money to access political power. While it doesn't sound noble—because it isn't!—it's almost unavoidable because without the money, it's nearly impossible to get elected, let alone re-elected, or introduce or advance a bill through Congress. It's a sad fact that most lawmakers spend as much time asking for money than they do talking to constituents and legislating. (Google CBS News' "60 Minutes" segment on what's called Dialing for Dollars. *Whoa!*)

So, if you're seemingly terrific progressive senator casts a bizarre vote that seems to be an about-face on everything you love about them, poke around a bit. What industry is big in the state? What corporations support the economy? How sure is that senator's re-election? Need help finding that information? OpenSecrets.org is a powerful place to start. Go to the *Get Local!* link, and get a factsheet on your area. You can find out how much money there is, who is getting it, and where it's coming from. Feeling outraged? *Oh, there's so much more!* Don't forget to check out Action #71 to feed your outrage and learn ways to pushback against the all-mighty, often-ugly dollar! (And call that politician whose vote upset you. See Action #46 for help with that.)

33. Pitch in for your elevator pitch

Pretend that you have to convince someone of your opinion on a subject in the time it takes to ride down together in an elevator. Salespeople call this technique an "elevator pitch." For that pitch to go well, you have to pick only the *most important, most persuasive* parts of your argument. You also have to have it ready at an *instant*. In other words, when you have those important few minutes to state your case, you do *not* want to be stammering and blanking out (believe us ... we've learned this one the hard, painful way!).

Write down your elevator pitch—your most persuasive case for your opinion—and then practice, practice, practice. Don't stop until you have a one-, three-, and five-minute spiel. Rehearse in a mirror and visualize yourself making a calm, practiced, smooth pitch to convince others about what must be done and about why it can't be ignored. You can use your pitch at parties when people ask why you think what's going on in the country is such a big deal. Or use it to help explain yourself if you ever speak to a congressperson (see Action #51) or at a public meeting on the topic (see Action #49).

May We Suggest ...

Mirrors are great for rehearsing our activism. (Recording yourself on your cell phone also works great!) Use the mirror or your recording to practice your elevator pitch. And while you're there, you can also imagine yourself speaking truth to power (try saying things like "I respectfully disagree and do find that we still have a problem with racism in this country"). Or imagine stepping up to say something when you see something ("Hey, it's not OK to talk like that" is a great start). And while you're talking to yourself, take a second to tell yourself that you are amazing for caring enough to change the world.

34a. Confronting apathy without getting apoplectic

If you haven't figured it out already, activist, crafting your message is really only half the battle. You'll soon see that most people don't really care about this stuff you feel so passionately about. It is frustrating, and it's all too easy to get emotional when trying to get them to care. Don't get us wrong: we get emotional. (We get PISSED OFF as well!) This is important stuff, and apathy is *infuriating.*

Apathy is super privileged, too. People get uncomfortable talking about privilege. Keeping calm helps. It helps YOU. You have a lot of work to do, and we need you to pace yourself. Try calmly explaining why you care about a given issue or candidate (start with your elevator pitch, Action #33) and begin to slowly connect your audience to your cause. It isn't easy, but it's important and you're up for the challenge! If you don't succeed the first time, try again. And again. Your friends will get tired of hearing you talk about the issues, about your concerns, about their privilege. That's okay. Be redundant. It's important.

Repetition is important. Making connections for them is important. Keep trying. Apathy is a powerful tool of power. And you're no tool!

34b. Arguing effectively

You will also meet people who disagree with you almost entirely. Some of these people will have a very different, but thoughtfully reasoned, perspective. Be open-minded in your discussions with them. If they can disagree with you respectfully, you can do the same. Finding common ground isn't difficult where there is respect. Here are some helpful tips:

- **Listen.** *Really* listen—don't just wait for the other person to stop talking. What they are saying gives you important intel on their values, which will help you figure out how to proceed in your discussion.
- **Appeal to their "values," not your own.** If you're talking to someone arguing against same-sex marriage (seriously!?), don't jump all over them about being unfair (no matter how much you want to). Simply put: fairness isn't what they morally care about. However, if you can point out how the evolving attempt at ensuring civil liberties for all is uniquely American and a celebration of how deeply we honor freedom, you just may get them to listen further because you are appealing to a common set of values that we all share.

- **Keep calm, don't carry on.** You can't control the other person's responses or emotions, but you can control yours. Keep calm. If the other person doesn't follow your lead and keep a cool head, don't hesitate to walk away.
- **Think win-win.** Talking to people you don't agree with is a lot easier if you can assume that they're coming from a place of good intentions. Don't focus on winning the argument. Instead, look for common ground and *genuinely* listen to understand.
- **Know your goals.** Sometimes you're trying to convince someone to see your viewpoint; sometimes you're trying to get them to change their mind; and sometimes you're just speaking up to balance out their hateful speech. Know what you're going for, and adjust yourself accordingly.

34c. Don't feed the trolls. They bite ... and suck.

Alas, you will find people who don't know a lot about the issues but will be very vocal nonetheless. Some of those people will parrot what they've heard somewhere (even if it's 100 percent false), and some of those people will proudly hold views that are hateful, scared, and completely ignorant. Obviously, these are the hardest cases. *How do we politely say this?* At best these people are morons. (Ok, we didn't try all that hard to be polite.) At worst, these are who Hillary Clinton quite justifiably called the deplorables ... and deplorable they are. These aren't arguments worth engaging in. In fact, these are the kind of arguments that can escalate out of control quickly.

The trick is to spot the trolly deplorables quickly. It takes practice, but it will save you lots of time and energy and help keep you safe. If you cannot trust that the other person shows a willingness to play fair, trust your instincts and avoid the conversation. Someone has to stand up to these fools, for sure, but assess your risk before volunteering. You might try stating your argument once, then moving on. Or it might mean biting your tongue and walking away. It's not defeat: it's refusing to engage with someone not ready to listen ... or worse. Engaging in a month-long social media "fight" with your aunt's boyfriend over gun control might seem satisfying, but—believe us!—once you realize how unprepared he is to inch away from his set arguments, it'll get old real fast! Save your energy; you'll need it elsewhere.

35. Write a letter to the editor

Every paper has a section where it publishes what are called "letters to the editor." These letters are where members of the public write in to state their opinion about a current event or a concern of the community or something along those lines. Letters to the editor have become an important part of the resistance movement because the letters allow average people to spread their concerns far and wide in a way outside of social media.

Letters to the editor are short (keep it to fewer than 175 words) and timely (so don't write about something that happened a month ago). Keep it fast-paced and sharply worded, with facts mixed in with your arguments. (For example, you might say something like, "While some people call undocumented people in the United States ugly things like freeloaders, the Social Security Administration says that undocumented workers contributed $13 billion in payroll taxes in 2010, which is the most recent year available. So, in fact, undocumented workers are not only adding to a local economy by spending the money they make at their jobs, but they also are often paying taxes as well.")

Every newspaper has a different deadline or different rules and formats that they want for their letters, so be sure to check out each paper's policy before you write your letter. (For information on finding your local news sources, turn to Action #43.)

36. Get trendy

If there's anything your generation knows better than anyone else, it's social media. Put that knowledge to good use as part of your activism and as part of your work to spread your message. Work together with friends to get a hashtag trending to help push what you are concerned about to the forefront of social media. You can use an app such as Thunderclap to make the hashtags appear simultaneously and help your message gain even more momentum.

If you need some guidance on how best to make your tweets count, #TheResistance Tweetsheets (resistancetweetsheets.wordpress.com) is dedicated to mobilizing, empowering, and guiding Twitter users to be an effective part of the movement. And if you need some models on activists who make great use of social media, look to DiDi Delgado (@TheDiDiDelgado) and Zach Anner (@Zachanner).

Be aware as you move forward with your social media activism that there can be some pitfalls, including various shades of online harassment such as doxxing and swatting. Some easier ways to protect yourself from these include using original passwords for every account and Googling yourself and eliminating any excess personal information online (try justdelete.me to help with that).

37. Make a meme that's not about me-me-me

Create a meme that reminds people of the importance of your message. Pick your passion and start brainstorming what you want to tell others about it. (And, yeah, make it really sarcastic because—let's be honest—that makes it a lot more fun!) You might go with something like: "Another severe storm destroys lives and homes? Tell me again how global warming isn't real." Or "An average of seven U.S. kids or teens are killed by guns each day. Exactly when is it that I'm supposed to get mad about that?" Then find a good still from a TV show or movie and use an online meme generator or meme app to create your masterpiece. Share your finished product with the world. (Or at least text it to friends!)

38. Don't. Just. Click.

Signing and clicking an online petition gives us all that little burst of accomplishment that our brains love. Alas, online petitions aren't usually effective in actually bringing about change. (Even worse—sometimes our satisfied brain tricks us into thinking that our work is done after we click and makes us stop looking for ways to help.)

Fight the urge to just click to make yourself feel better. The resistance needs boots on the ground and hearts in the battles. Pledge more than just some clicks: pledge to engage yourself meaningfully in the resistance, and go out there and work to make a change in the real world. (As in—ahem—work to do some of the actions in this very book.) If you like the idea of a petition, check out the next action.

39. Start a paper petition of your own

Just because online petitions have a bad reputation doesn't mean that they aren't effective. Paper petitions have been an important part of the political process since our country's beginning. In fact, the petition clause of the First Amendment of the Constitution guarantees the right of the people "to petition the Government for a redress of grievances." (Wouldn't that be more interesting set to rap? Where's Lin-Manuel Miranda when you need him?)

If there's a local issue you are upset about (petitions are most effective for local issues), then by all means start a paper petition. (This action will include some contact with other people, so be sure to keep your safety in mind.) The petition should state your concern formally, such as: "We the below signed are upset that the community center hours have been cut and would like to see the hours increased to their former level." Have people print their name and address and add their signature. Then—*and this is the important part*—figure out who should get the petition and schedule a meeting to present it to them. At the meeting, point out how many people share your concerns, explain how you would like to see the problem resolved, and advise what action steps are needed. The petition may not change anything, but at least you will learn a lot about the democratic process while doing it, which automatically counts as a win in our book.

Go the Extra Step

Be sure to write a news release (see Action #40) about your petition and send it off to all of your local papers, both big and small. This will help to further get the word out about your concerns. You could write one news release about how you're collecting signatures and a second news release after you present the petition. Good luck!

40. Whatever you do, make it news! Learn to write a news release

A news release—also called a media advisory or media release—is like giving a media outlet a heads-up that you're about to do something awesome. It lets the media know the Who, the What, the Where, the When, the Why, and the How of an event that you're planning or participating in. You can find contact information on media websites or on their social media. Send each email individually. Use the same release for each but don't CC them. (If possible, send it to a specific reporter rather than just a general info address.)

You can also send out releases after an action to let the media know you did something newsworthy that they should cover or come interview you about. Include a summary of what happened and—*important tip*—be sure to includes pictures and/or video of the event to make covering the story more appealing.

Releases sound (and are) official but are really quite simple. You can find a basic template with an Internet search. Be sure to include your name and contact info (OK it with your adult). Some other hints:

- *Include your age!* People like to think young people don't care; prove otherwise.
- *Be timely.* Send one about a week before the event (or no more than a day after the event).

- *Make sure it's news.* You sending a postcard to your congressperson is not news; you and 50 of your young friends caring enough to come together to write and send postcards is.
- *Put important stuff first.* Think of a release like a newspaper article and mention the most important info first.
- *Be concise.* It should be no longer than a brief page at most and can even be in a short Who/What/Why/When/Where/How bulleted format.

CHAPTER FOUR

Stand in the Place Where You Live

Actions to Act Locally

• • •

"You can't solve all the problems of the world,
but each day you can do something."

—JANE GOODALL,
British primatologist, anthropologist,
and UN Messenger of Peace

Dear Friend,

Think globally, act locally was this fresh new take (at least for me) back when I was in college. And I'll be honest: I kind of thought it was a bunch of B.S. Sure, local issues matter, but the real power so clearly seemed to be in D.C., not in my town.

Yeesh, was I ever wrong! The local is where it's *at*. It's the building blocks for *all* things political, for goodness sake, and I somehow totally missed it! If you want systemic change, start local. If you want to try to make your city, town, or neighborhood a better place, start local. If you want to try to make a difference on a national topic you feel passionately about (say, voter's rights or immigrant rights), start local.

Notice I said *try*. Take it from someone who's had her activist heart broken a time or ten trying to make a difference locally: local opposition to change can be ... vigorous. So make the *journey* (not the end result) your focus. This chapter is all about that personal, local journey and learning how best to navigate it. The work might be hard, and the road might be long and not end exactly where you wished it would, but—with practice—you can learn to take heart in the fact that you are acting to create the kind of world that *you* want to live in. And that's a pretty powerful statement.

Be the change!
Kerri

41. Where do you live?

Before you can act locally, you must first have a clear understanding of what your "local" is like. In fact, you're going to want a few opinions on this, so you're sure you have a well-rounded viewpoint. But first start by describing your community on a piece of paper.

Write down who lives there. Is it racially or culturally diverse? Is it economically diverse (meaning, are there lots of different income levels)? Is there a wide range of ages (not just mostly young families or older seniors, for example)? Are most people one type of religion, or are many different beliefs represented? Do most people feel one way or another about politics, or is it a mix of feelings?

Next, think about the community as a whole. What are its strengths? What are its resources? What is really nice about your community, and what is not so great about it? Think about the community's challenges. Are those the strengths and challenges of everyone in the area or of only some? Why is—or isn't—that the case?

Now it's time to pull in some outside experts: other locals. Ask trusted, knowledgeable adults their thoughts about the community. Do those opinions match yours? Look for other perspectives around you— Jewish, Muslim, atheists, older people, LGBTQ people, people from the disabled community, people with more money, people with less money, immigrants and children of immigrants, etc. Listen out for these voices, and see if those opinions differ from what you have already found. Is your perspective on where you live changing, shifting, growing? Now you really know where you live. Let's move on.

42. Take one small step where you live

Think about the community challenges you listed in the previous action. Is there a small step you could take in addressing one? It might be something as small as picking up the litter on your block or something as big as helping those who can't afford healthy groceries. Make a plan to put that small step from thought into action. Tip: break the plan into small parts to help you accomplish it more easily.

Even easier: look around to see if anyone is already working on this problem in your area. If a person or group is already addressing it, take their expert advice! Reach out and ask them what you can do to help the effort. (And then take them at their word and follow through on what they say they need: Buying jars of peanut butter to take to the food bank is great, but if what they really need is toothpaste and toothbrushes, you're not helping as much as you could.)

May We Suggest …

Setting goals or plans are always so fun and interesting … at first. Then it's all too easy to shuffle them to the back of your leaky brainpan and forget all about them. Help yourself out by creating an action plan that you can follow. Keep it specific: plan, for example, "I will pick up the litter on my block every Saturday" versus a vague "I want to do something about the litter in my community." And keep it realistic: "I want to ask my library to set up a conversation table where Spanish-speakers can come practice their English" versus the too-big "I want to help undocumented people practice their English so they can negotiate the U.S. system better."

43. Support very local news

It's important to think about where you get your news. The Internet, the 24-hour cable news cycle, and the consolidation of media ownership has made it easy to get news every moment of the day or night, but it is important to remember that quantity of news does not mean quality of news or completeness of coverage.

It's ironic but while it's getting easier to see what's happening nationally and internationally, it's also getting harder to know what's happening in your own area (outside of social media, that is). You may have a local paper—and some lucky places still do—but they are most likely struggling financially. That paper may do the best it can to keep up with the news in the region and may even include some pretty serious investigative journalism that looks deeply at problems and issues that most affect where you live. This is important to support! If you are lucky enough to have a smaller paper for your town (or for your neighborhood in bigger cities), buy the paper from time to time or purchase a subscription if you can afford it. Either way, look at the paper's advertisers and mention that you saw them there the next time you are in that business.

A note: many "local" papers are now owned by large companies headquartered across the country. Be sure to check to see if your paper still seems to have a local edge in its coverage, or if it's mostly stuff from somewhere else. If you have a few local choices, buy the one that is locally owned—especially if their coverage is better focused on your area.

44. Start a zine

Zines (pronounced *zeens*) were all the rage back in the day when the Internet was just something from a science fiction novel and computers stayed on desks, not in pockets. (Think waayyyy back to the cutting-edge technology of, say, "Saved by the Bell" time.) Back then, it was hard for the average person to get her voice heard. People couldn't easily make and distribute their own movies or self-publish books. And they certainly didn't have social media to amplify their voice. Zines gave people outside the mainstream media a platform.

These often-punchy, intentionally-low-tech DIY pamphlets are written and illustrated by hand, copied on a machine, and stapled with a good old-fashioned stapler. The best part? Zines are about whatever you, the publisher, want them to be. Food? Sure. Siblings? Yep. Emotions. Fine. Politics? Oh, hecks *yeah*! Start a zine by yourself or with friends about what you see going on in the world. Make copies. Spread your message. Lather, rinse, repeat.

45. Call your rep

Let's face it: emails are easier than phone calls, and politicians know this. A quick phone call will always carry more weight to a politician than an email, so Be. Sure. To. Make. The. Calls. Once you've made your first call, you won't believe how easy it is (it really is practically as easy as an email).

Find the numbers for the politicians who represent you at a national level (in the Senate and the House of Representatives) and at the state level (the governor and state congresspeople), and program them into your phone so it's easy to call every day if you wish; see Action #7 for help finding the numbers. (They may have several numbers listed. Any one of them will work for a call.)

It might help to prepare a script, but your phone call need only be a few seconds long, such as: "Hi. I live in [your city name here], and I want to urge [politician's name here] to vote against the new health care law that has been in the news." That's really all you need. If you're feeling like you want to say more, you can add a short-and-sweet explanation: "It is unfair and creates a burden for the sick."

The person taking the call may ask for your name and zip code or might just say something like, "I will pass that along. Thank you for calling." And—*tah-dah!*—that's it. You hang up and go about your busy life, knowing that you had your say. (If you feel particularly passionate on a topic, you can also visit those who represent you; see Action #51.)

Now get out there and say it loud, say it proud: tell others that you made a call, explain how easy it is, and urge them to call as well. Include contact information for the politicians they should call to make it extra-easy for them.

May We Suggest ...

If you're feeling unsure of when to call or what to say to them, Indivisible (www.indivisibleguide.com), Action for a Better Tomorrow (actionforabettertomorrow.org), and The 65 (thesixtyfive.org) are wonderful action groups that provide pointers on who to call and what to say. Or the Action Hub at What Do I Do About Trump? (whatdoidoabouttrump.com/action-hub/) gathers together ideas from many different useful sources.

46. Show you're paying attention close to home

Don't forget that it's not just the folks in Washington, D.C., who are making laws that affect our lives. The resistance needs to be working at all levels—not just nationally. We have politicians at the state level (governors, state congresspeople), the county level (commissioners, etc.), and the city level (mayors, city council members, park district board members, etc.).

Find out who these people are in your area and send them a letter or make a phone call to them explaining what kinds of actions you would like to see them taking. (Tip: decide before you dial what it is you want to say, and keep phone calls short and sweet. If you're going to call often, it can be valuable to start learning the names of the people who answer the phones. It's also a great idea to keep a record of your calls and the responses you get.)

47. Post some snail mail

Postcards are mighty tools. They are simple, relatively inexpensive, and can be used for practically every action. They can help you blow off some steam (but they shouldn't be belligerent), they can state your position and urge others toward the same viewpoint, or they can just say thank you. A postcard is a quick, concrete action that feels empowering because it *is* empowering: you are quite literally putting your words and thoughts out there. Buy your postcards already made or design them, print them, or upcycle them from existing paper (be sure to check the USPS website for size rules for postcards).

Put the already-stamped postcards somewhere handy to encourage yourself (and others) to write them regularly. Stack a pile of empty, pre-stamped postcards on your dinner table for when someone has a quick moment. Put some by where you do homework and dash off a quick note every few days. Postcards are your friends! (Believe it or not, the price of sending postcards can add up quickly, so be sure to check out Chapter 9 to help to fund your stamp stockpile!)

48. Give the gift of activism

Have like-minded friends or family members? Celebrate their birthdays by slipping a customized list of the person's representatives (local, state, and national) and contact information in a birthday card. (Bonus: you get to bring back the time-honored tradition of giving paper cards!) Include a short script (*My name is ___, and I'm from ___. I'm calling to express my opposition to ___. Thank you.*) and some encouragement that it really is that easy to call. If you have the means, you can include a few pre-addressed, pre-stamped postcards as well.

49. Go to a local meeting

Here's an idea for a night that will be a gaggle of giggles: attend a local board or council meeting. (Don't forget the party hats!) If you search online, you can easily find the dates for public meetings of your local school board, your city council, your library board, your park district board, and so on. Sure, they might be dry and kind of boring (OK, we promise they'll be dry and boring), but you'll get to see the people who are making decisions (and how few of them there are holding the power) and what the local process of governing looks like. Maybe even more important: you'll get to hear what other citizens are concerned about in your area. Most meetings have a public comment period at the beginning of the meeting where locals can come air their concerns or their kudos or whatever else might be on their minds. Maybe someday soon you'll be inspired to stand up and speak as well.

50. Volunteer for a campaign

It's hard to think about a better way to learn about politics and the election system than by volunteering for a campaign, whether it is for state senate, a governor, school board, or even president. About six months before the next election, start looking for a candidate whose policies you agree with. Ask to make an appointment to meet with her or with a campaign manager or adviser. If you like what that person has to say, ask how you can help the campaign. (Remember to think about those skills you brainstormed in Action #1 and be specific on what you have to offer.) Your candidate might not win the election, but you will win a lot of knowledge ... no matter what.

51. (Try to) meet a member of Congress

Did you know that all members of Congress have at least one (and sometimes several) local offices in their states? The politicians themselves aren't always in the office, but staffers keep regular hours. Their job is to listen to the people and then pass along that information to the boss (a k a the congressperson). And when visitors care enough to actually show up at the office, that shows real commitment to the message and scores extra points.

Look up the office closest to you for a Senator or representative in Congress. You can either schedule an appointment to meet with the politician about a certain issue (it's not easy to do but it's not unheard of either). Or simply drop by during office hours and meet a staffer. (Tip: call ahead just to be double-sure a staffer will be there when you arrive.) Once you're there, either thank the politician for supporting what you believe in or express your concerns about the direction the congressperson's support is headed. (Another tip: hone your elevator pitch—Action #33—before you go).

As an extra-certain way to make sure your voice is heard, bring along a letter with a specific call to action for the congressperson. Present this letter to the staffer or the congressperson during your visit, and—finally—make sure you emphasize as you leave that this is the action you'd like for him or her to take.

For example, you might write a letter about your support for the rights of transgendered people (be sure to include specifics on why exactly you support your cause) and call on the politician to do the same. (If you know of any specific bills coming up that concern you, it's even better if you can include how you want him or her to vote on that bill.)

May We Suggest ...
If you want to look extra polished and adult-y and make this action extra-effective, be sure to send a thank-you note to the office after your visit. Thank them for their time and remind them of what stance you would like to see them taking.

Go the Extra Step
Write a letter to the editor of your big and small local papers talking about your visit and how you urged the politician representing your area to take a certain stance. Explain

specifically why you think this stance is of utmost importance to your region and our country. (For more on letters to the editor, see Action #35.) Don't forget to state your age!

52. When where you live, well, kinda sucks

You might be one of those lucky people who strolls down the streets of your community feeling safe in your viewpoint and excited about where the future is heading and glad to be part of a place that just "gets it." Or you might live in an area where you don't fit in, or even want to fit in, and you constantly fantasize about fleeing for someplace where you can truly belong. If where you live and what you feel is more like the second one, obviously don't give up on your beliefs ... but don't give up on where you live just yet either.

Work where you live to do what you can, when you can. Look for the good, or look for the people who are working for good and lend them your time and your talents. It may not be a left-leaning cause called Progressive Movements R Us, but there will be *someplace* where you can put your belief in humanity into action—a food bank, a women's shelter, a charity for children with special needs....

You may be thinking, *What? Work for this place? No way! I'm out of here the second I can leave.* You know your life better than we do, and far be it for us to talk you out of your feelings. But keep in mind that this will always be the place you grew up, and you will always have that connection to it (even if it *is* a conflicted relationship!). If you can't try today, how about tomorrow (or sometime down the road) ... if even from a distance? Do what you can, do what you need to, and commit to working in the future for something that might help another kid who may be feeling stuck like you.

PART TWO
ACTIVISM GETS REAL

• • •

"Our speaking out will irritate some people,
get us called bitchy or hypersensitive and
disrupt some dinner parties. And then our
speaking out will permit other women to
speak, until laws are changed and lives are
saved and the world is altered forever."

—AUDRE LORDE,
POET AND ACTIVIST

CHAPTER FIVE

United We Stand

Actions to Create a More Fair World

• • •

"The trouble is that once you see it, you can't unsee it. And once you've seen it, keeping quiet, saying nothing, becomes as political an act as speaking out. There's no innocence. Either way, you're accountable."

—ARUNDHATI ROY,

AUTHOR

Dear Activist,

I'm hoping I'm too old to write this letter. If you consider yourself progressive already, chances are you can teach me a thing or two about the following chapter on building alliances—true alliances, not just ones of political expedience. (For god's sake, I was in college before I met an openly out gay person! The depiction of women and people of color in television are still wrought with stereotypes. Can you imagine what I watched? And my parents, proud liberals, never challenged the stereotypes or worried about how I might internalize the messages.)

If you read through the chapter and think, *Yup, that's about right, I agree,* please drop me an email at joanna@ wakeriseresist.com so I can jump up and down, follow you on Instagram, friend you on Facebook, and genuinely feel better about the future of this country and all of civilization.

If you read this chapter and feel uncomfortable or defensive or even angry, write me a letter to complain. I can take it. I'd even be honored! (Maybe I'm not as old as I thought!) This chapter is meant to challenge your understanding of your racism, your sexism, your patriotism, and your privilege. Martin Luther King Jr. said, "Shallow understanding from people of good will is more frustrating than absolute misunderstanding from people of ill will." I hope you'll read this chapter and deepen your understanding.

Anxiously awaiting your reply,
Joanna

53. Understand your intersectionality

You can't throw a rock on the Internet these days without hitting a discussion of intersectionality. And while the name sounds fancy and the talk can be pretty heady and intellectual and all *what-the-what-now?*, it really just means that you cannot pull apart any of the oppressive parts of our world. Racism, sexism, homophobia, Islamophobia, xenophobia, or any of those other delightful -isms or -phobias that weigh our country down like an anchor tied around our collective necks do not exist alone; they are part of an interconnected web of horrors. So if a white transgender woman were discussing sexism, she would be coming at it from the additional angle of being LGBTQ but also from the privilege (see Action #57) of a white person. She is not just a woman in a vacuum experiencing sexism, but a woman with other issues and traits that impact her life and make some things easier in general society and some things harder in general society.

Think about your own labels: Latinx, Autistic, Gay, Fat, Male, Jewish, Able-bodied.... Do any of your labels completely define you? How do you work for the advancement of any one of your "tribes" when each of us belongs to more than one? How do your tribes intersect, and how do they all work together and individually to inform who you are and what your life experiences are?

54. Understand *our* intersectionality

Just as each person has intersectionality of their labels (see Action #53), so too does our country have intersectionality of class, race, gender, sexuality, ability, age, and more. To truly transform ourselves into the powerhouse alliance that our movement needs, we must work to see these intersections and understand how they affect the country as a whole and every single person within it. These intersections come together and come apart in the country's power structures and often keep us from seeing—really, truly *seeing*—the realities of other people.

Some people—due to how their identities have intersected (or not intersected) with power—have been rendered nearly invisible and feel justifiably resentful. We must work constantly to allow all members to have an equal seat at the table. Intersectionality is such a wonderful term and an even more glorious concept for us to live up to: we in this country intersect, just as our dreams and goals and decision-making should also intersect.

55. Grow Your Growth Mindset

You've probably heard the term "growth mindset" about a zillion times at school and it may be approaching the Charlie Brown teacher *wah-wah-wah-wah* noise, but that doesn't mean it's still not a really kick-butt concept to live by—even an exciting concept to live by. In fact we two writers credit our growth mindsets with changing our lives in a good way this past year (rather than the plentiful crummy ways our worlds have changed since November 2016). If you had told us we were racist back in early 2016, our backs would have stiffened, and we would have called you out. *What? Us? Racist! Never! Bite your tongue, and slap yourself while you're at it!*

But thanks to a growth mindset, we now—after months of thinking and reading and discussing and learning and debating—have been able to grow our understanding of the world and ourselves to where we understand that, yes, we are racist. (We're not *proud* to say it, of course—who would be?—but we are *honest* enough to say it.)

Like it or not, we all live in a profoundly racist culture, and we all participate in its power structures. And that's the root of the casual racism we have internalized and denied ourselves from seeing. We now understand that our kneejerk response of *racist-who-me??* denied the racism that existed in our own personal worlds and in our own internalized biases. What a shame! We missed out on working on our own racist thinking and on more effectively combatting this country's everyday racism. We now allow ourselves to see the world for what it is even when it's not the picture we want it to be. Challenging our thinking has made us better activists.

Don't make our mistake: don't age yourself into a fixed way of thinking without realizing it. For many Americans, our notions of gender, race/ethnicity, culture, sexuality, identity have grown by leaps and bounds over the last two decades. Keep your wonder and willingness to confront yourself open to these kinds of new ideas. The world is changing and evolving—leave yourself open to changing and evolving with it.

56. Lessons from the Women's March on Washington

The time leading up to the Women's March on Washington was an education for many white women—and yet another example of the all-too-familiar exclusion experienced by marginalized peoples. As white women rushed to the resistance, many were stunned, hurt, and angered by the reluctance of numerous marginalized women and femme people to join *this* march. Some white women—including these authors—learned a lot those months: lessons they should have already known, to be honest. Others didn't learn and haven't still.

But more white people are beginning to listen. The needle on the country's awareness, understanding, and acceptance has moved since Donald Trump was elected President of the United States. The fact that the shift in the national conversation did not happen sooner or without considerable aggressive pushback from white liberals proves the point: until white, gender-conforming women had *their* privilege threatened by a maniacal, anti-women scumbag of a president, they were ignorant, disinterested, and downright dismissive of what marginalized people have been saying for decades. The notion that the dismissed would simply line up to march on behalf of the privileged (again!) was too much to ask, and many marginalized women stayed away from the march.

The Women's March on Washington worked to address and recover from these concerns and was an important experience for millions of people (across the spectrum). Powerful women (representative of that beautiful spectrum) stepped up to offer their knowledge, experience, and leadership skills. They produced a platform that is fantastic, even if we are only dreaming of living up to the ideals it presents. Read the Guiding Vision and Definition of Principles of the Women's March on Washington (go to www.womensmarch.com/mission/ and click on the PDF link). The march organizers created a loving, inclusive glimpse at a world where no person is left behind to wander the wilderness on her own.

Then read the criticism and experiences of the people who marched with reservations or who chose not to march at all. (May we suggest our contributing editor Jessica Davis's "Why I Ain't Marchin'" on Medium as an excellent place to start? Search for the title at Medium or go to medium.com/@jessicadavis_96034/why-i-aint-marchin-ef0897face43.) Their absence is as powerful a statement as any and must be understood in order to collectively march this country forward—finally.

57. See privilege

Time to revisit privilege (Action #11). In fact, young progressive, your job is to continue to keep the discussion about privilege center-stage and moving forward. To do so, you must first—if you haven't already—examine your own privilege and see what it provides you. (Google "MIT privilege checklists" to help you better understand white privilege, able-bodied privilege, social class privilege, male privilege, and heterosexual privilege.)

Yes, it can be overwhelming at best (and scary at worst) to open yourself up to seeing your own privilege, but you are the captain of a growth mindset (see Action #55), and you know that you don't have to fear change. We all have some privilege, so go ahead and let yourself see it.

Once you have examined your privilege, let history help you see its roots. To do so, study the history of whatever group/s you belong to (black, able-bodied, male, etc.) and see how much control this group has historically had over its own destiny. If the groups you identify with have little privilege, you will learn that these disadvantages are part of a complicated web that keeps power in few hands (and mostly hands that don't look like yours!). Recognizing this may make you feel helpless, but when you start seeing it, you can begin working to actually dismantle the system and can also begin removing any of its bull-pucky that you might have internalized. (Word to the wise: never internalize bull-pucky; it's highly unappetizing.)

58. Practice seeing privilege

Privilege is one of those crazy things where it's hidden in plain sight for those who have it. Unfortunately, just knowing privilege exists is not enough to start noticing it. Believe it or not, it takes practice to see (and constant vigilance to continue seeing it). Start off here with a little practice. Think about these scenarios and what they say about our society and the privilege within it:

- You are not Muslim, but you like to share your opinion on women wearing a hijab. (Is that yours to knowledgeably discuss? Don't speak for other people's experiences.)
- Your one Muslim friend says it's okay to joke about hijabs, so now you—who are not Muslim—feel free to start joking about it. (Yeah, no. One person from a culture is not allowed to give an okay for a whole culture.)
- You are a white woman who has read several articles on Black Lives Matter and attend your first local meeting. You feel well informed enough to add to the debate at the meeting. (No. Just listen. One article or even five does not make you an expert; see Action #18.)
- You see a young black man hailing a cab and pause to think about how hard it will probably be for him to get a ride. (Now you're getting there. You're starting to think about others' realities.)
- Your white female friend says a white male teacher always rests his hands on her shoulder, and it makes her uncomfortable. You tell her that she's being too sensitive, and

it just means that he thinks she's smart. (Don't explain away female discomfort over unasked-for male attention. Females get to say what makes them uncomfortable.)

- Your team's mascot isn't an accurate representation of a Native American, but you tell people that it's a school tradition and that it's not supposed to be offensive—it's supposed to honor the native tradition. (Have you ever noticed that when people say "no offense" before something, it's usually deeply offensive? "No offense, but you look really stupid in that shirt." Just because you say "no offense" doesn't make it better, so stop pretending you get to decide if the mascot is offensive or not. That mascot dehumanizes whole groups of people and belittles some really atrocious injustices against that population, so—no offense—but your mascot sucks and is an example of privilege in action.)

59. Wake up and see color

For race relations to get any better in this country, let's start with one radical but important clarification. It's not race relations that need to improve, it's *racism* that needs to stop. Stop right here, and let that soak in: *it's racism that needs to stop.*

In truth, race isn't really a thing. Race is a false construct used to separate people into groups so that a dominant group can hold its power. Racism, sadly, *is* totally a real thing. To end racism, white people—especially white, thoughtful, progressive people—must think beyond "we're all equal" and examine how and why racism still exists when it is so clearly disgusting. They also need to consider how they (prepare to get a little uncomfortable here, white folk) benefit from keeping it that way.

For decades now, it's been common practice for white people to avoid seeing color in an effort to show that race "doesn't matter" to us. (We're intentionally going to use "we" and "us" for the rest of this action because *we*—the writers—are white and understand that *we*—white liberals—still have work to do.). The idea is that if we're "color blind" when it comes to race that we minimize racism and allow people to stop judging others by the color of their skin. This simply hasn't worked. In fact, it's actually made racism *worse.* By not seeing color, we are more apt to "not see" the real obstacles, real struggles, and *real* racism people of color experience every day. The intention might feel okay and even honorable, but the impact has been devastating. White people have "moved on" while happily humming a tune, but the world has not moved on at all, leaving people of color to fight without allies.

The truth is, we need to see color. We need to wake up and see that racism still exists. We might like to think that we've personally risen above racism, but that was a false "victory." Our task now is to get *in* the racism—see it, explore it, sit with it, get uncomfortable by the ugliness of it, and finally begin the work of dismantling it.

You may be thinking, *But, wait! I don't feel like a racist!* Of course you don't ... but you are. We all are. We're not even bothering to talk about the racists that everyone can see from a mile away by the filth and hate spewing from their mouths. You aren't that. But, if you are white and feeling a little uncomfortable (or straight up angry) right now, we get it. It is uncomfortable to see your place—no matter how accidental—in the country's epidemic of racism. Incidentally, keep in mind that your white-person discomfort about racism isn't the point of any of this. The conversation shouldn't be even a little about *your* comfort level. Read this section again, remembering that white people make up the dominant culture and have most of the power in this country (and read Action #11 on privilege if you haven't already). And while not every white person thinks, feels, or does have the power they need, they do have a level of privilege that can't be denied.

60. Of course you're a feminist!

Let's face it: men have been coasting on a pretty sweet gig for the last, oh, few thousand years or so as they have dominated politics and culture and pretty much locked everyone else out until very recently. Our culture has followed suit, privileging men over women—even if only in our own internalized biases. Bah. Enough of that crap already. If you're reading this book we think it's pretty safe to say that you believe women are as important as men. Right? Tah-dah! Guess what? You're a feminist!

People who are against feminism say the craziest things to make feminism seem bad. Let us assure you: It isn't. Feminism can be boiled down to this: do you believe in equality for women? Yes? Bam! You're a feminist, despite what anyone else might try to make you believe. Welcome to a pretty wonderful club of people of many genders who believe in equality.

OK, so now that you know you're a feminist: say it loud, say it proud. It is on the rest of us to speak up for women's equality and feminism and counteract the message that some people are trying to spread about what feminism means. Don't be quiet: talk about your feminism to friends and family. Proudly label yourself a feminist. (Darn right, you are one!) Speak out to others around you when you see sexism on TV and in movies and hear it in songs. Shout it from the rooftops when you see the ridiculous pressures that ads puts on women and girls. (We assure you—it's not hard to find sexism in the media!)

Also important: speak out when you see sexism in real life as well (especially microaggressions; see Action #61). It is not OK for expectations and opportunities to be different for people based on gender. Make your voice heard, and educate others about why the fight for equality is far from over.

61. Be mindful of microaggressions

If sexism (or racism, for that matter) were always obvious, it would be much easier to fight. We'd immediately know it was wrong if a teacher outright said that girls weren't good at math or if a job openly stated that it was for men only. While that kind of sexism (and, again, racism) does exist, it's not the only way inequality is out there. Instead, what most often keeps women down are microaggressions, which are casual and subtle acts of discrimination. For example, what if a teacher only ever called on boys to answer the math questions? Isn't that sending a message that math is just for males?

There are many classic sexist microaggressions. For example, when women/femme people are called "pushy" or "bossy" (or something even more rude) for speaking aggressively, but men/masculine people who speak the same way are applauded for being "assertive." This microaggression tells girls and women that it's not OK for them to speak up and be a leader. Some other important issues to be mindful of:

- When a male explains something to a female that she obviously already knows (and might have even already said), it's a sign to the female that her thoughts don't count for much. (People like to call this one *mansplaining*. We like to call it annoying as #$%@.)
- When someone is called "too sensitive" or "politically correct" for pointing out inequality, it's a way to make people feel like they're overreacting as well as a way to silence those people. (It's like saying, "Just shut up and take it.")
- When female contributions, ideas, or thinking get overshadowed by people's opinions of her clothing, it says what's

outside is more important than how a woman thinks. (Like when female leaders make an amazing speech and then people say, "Her outfit was atrocious. She looked so old.")

Go the Extra Step

People and personalities we admire are often our first entry into thinking progressively and not just as our mass culture does. Do you have a feminist role model, someone who taught you to see women differently? Thank her (or him) for the guidance. She may not even think of herself as a feminist. If you don't feel like you have a role model like this in your life, vow right now to be the feminist mentor for someone who looks up to you.

62. Say no to xenophobia

Aside from the indigenous peoples of the country, the entire United States is made up of immigrants. (Pause here for a second to remember that a big part of our population was forced here as immigrants through slavery and another part was already here and forced off their lands.) It's something that has long been part of our prided, true-blue, stars-and-stripes American story—that we are plucky immigrants who came here seeking a better life, that we were "longing to breathe free" and came and made it so. How ironic, then, that those in power have now decided to make it as American as apple pie to be openly hateful and racist and disgusting toward immigrants. *cough***hypocrites***cough* Add the

Islamophobia element hurled at Muslim immigrants, and, well, that's a hate sandwich that every American should be ashamed to call their own. This kind of xenophobia—hatred of immigrants—holds everyone back, not just the immigrants. Immigrants have added so much to our American culture: new words, new inventions, new music styles, new foods, new ideas … the list never ends. And that's not even to mention the mere fact that giving someone else the chance to start afresh, to breathe free is something that every righteous citizen should be proud to offer others.

63. It's the stupid economy, stupid

If you are lucky enough to have economic privilege, first take a second to thank your lucky stars because your life is and will be much easier for it. We are a country that likes to believe in the American Dream and equal opportunities for all, but the reality is far less rosy. Start thinking about all the ways that economic injustice affects people—people arrested and stuck in jail until trial because they can't afford bail, for example, or people whose unions have collapsed and are no longer making a solid wage. (If you are unsure about all of the ways that economic injustice occurs, go to TalkPoverty.org, a project of the Center for American Progress, for a view of the topic from many angles.)

Next move into action mode and start thinking about how you want to work for economic justice. You can join the fight for a higher minimum wage (Fight for $15 at fightfor15.org), join the movement for bail reform (the Southern Coalition for Social Justice, www.southerncoalition.org, is one place to do that), or work to make affordable housing available to all income brackets (see Action #77). People like to talk about the poor pulling themselves up "by their bootstraps," but always remember that it's impossible to do that when you have no feet. Commit yourself to helping to build this solid economic foundation for others.

64. Take a long, hard look at patriotism

Patriotism, or love of country, can be a beautiful, wondrous, powerful thing. But because we in the United States always like to make things super-sized (Super Big Gulp, anyone?), some Americans have come to believe that patriotism has to be *blind* love of country—of always thinking that it is *the* best and *the* most powerful and *the* most wonderful and *the* most righteous and *the* most just and that it never, ever needs to change or evolve. (Riiiiight. If that were true, we'd still have legal slavery, child factory workers, and only rich males voting.) Believing in America's "exceptionalism" isn't patriotism, it's nationalism. Nationalism is dangerous; it puts power and superiority above all else and encourages people to think in terms of us and them, as *with us* or *against us.*

True patriotism is seeing a country for how it really is—all of its powerful strengths, gorgeous possibilities, and worrisome weaknesses. Don't believe so much in anything that you can't see it for what it really is, even if that reality is messy or complicated or painful. Be a true patriot—not a nationalist—and know what you love and admire about your country, but also where it falls down on the job of living up to its ideals. You can be a patriot and be critical. In fact, you must be.

65. Be inclusive

Political correctness took a hit in the 2016 elections—as if using a way of speaking that includes all types of people is so controversial. As two people who grew up reading non-politically correct language, we can only assure you young'uns that you don't wanna go backward on this. (We had the "joys" of a childhood spent reading stuff like, "Each voter then casts his ballot for President," and having to wonder why we girls would be one of those voters casting *his* ballot. You'll notice that at some points in our book we're using *she* and *her* as our go-to one-size-fits-all pronoun to see what it's like from the other side—as in, "Each member of Congress cast her vote." It's jarring to see even for old feminists like us. Makes you wonder why *he* and *him* are supposed to be so much better!)

Be mindful of the power in your everyday language and work to make it inclusive and empowering to the many lovely peoples of this great nation. Rather than asking about someone's "mom and dad," for example, you might ask about "their parents" in case they have same-sex or trans parents. It's not so hard to set your table so everyone feels welcome.

66. Act your age

Everyone has their labels—you might be gay and white and West Coast suburban, or maybe you're straight and Latina and Southern rural. But as different as you all are, you all intersect at one important label: you're young. Your youth is where you overlap, and this is your strength, your common force.

Proudly act your age! Embrace your *youth culture*—the way you live, your values, behaviors, and the rules you have in common. Adults might regard you as not-fully-formed grown-ups, but they're (probably intentionally) not getting it. Understand the value of your youth (believe us, it goes fast!!) and exercise your collective power and youthful passions and energy! How? Well, far be it from *us* to tell *you* … but here's a start:

- Explore Youth Speaks (youthspeaks.org). Even if its programs are too far away or don't quite apply to you, you will certainly get inspired! (Young men of color, lend your voices to the powerful I Want to Live project: youthspeaks. org/iwanttolive.)
- Voices of Youth (www.voicesofyouth.org) sells itself as the online home for young people who actually do give a damn. 'Nuff said. Head yourself thataway.
- Read, write, and connect with other teens at Figment (figment. com), an awesome site for creative expression.
- Read the teen blog at the MET: www.metmuseum.org/ blogs/teen-blog.

- Figure it out by your-creative-savvy-thoughtful-selves! Do you have a friend who thinks about the world and its challenges like you do? (Yay!) Knock heads, keep talking, create, code, dream, idealize, Instagram, learn, jam, explore *your* way. Believe in yourself, in your unique way of looking at the world, and start applying your skills and talents now. #iamthefuture

CHAPTER SIX

Take Your Passion (and Make It Happen)

Actions to Follow Your Personal Interests

• • •

"We have to work for it! And
it's not going to be easy.
But guess what? It never was easy."

—JANET MOCK,
ACTIVIST

Dear Reader,

Look, if you're reading a book that is chockablock with actions for being part of the resistance, then I think it's safe to call you passionate in your activism. This chapter is all about how to take those passions—your environmentalism, your commitment to social justice, your belief in women's reproductive freedom, and so on—and put them to good, concrete use for the cause.

(Extra-credit points to those of you who recognized the "Flashdance" lyrics from our chapter title encouraging you to "make it happen"!)

When we started writing this chapter, we made that classic activist's mistake of thinking we had to reinvent the wheel: *I care about immigration and must now figure out—all on my own—a unique way that I can help!* Then we had the palm-to-the-forehead moment: There are already hardcore, honest-to-god, legit experts on each of these topics. What we needed to do is *connect* you to those like-minded groups.

So what we've done in this chapter is present you with 17 passion projects near and dear to the progressive heart, with a list of concrete, actionable ideas to help under each one. Some of these suggestions are individual actions to follow your passions; more often they are links to organizations that are already there, fighting the good fight. These groups are filled with knowledge on what needs to be done and have the savvy enough to know how to do it. They are desperately awaiting your passion and energy. Read on!

Yours in "Flashdance" and activism,
Kerri

67. Commit to justice. Period. (!)

A strong commitment to human rights, civil rights, and social and economic justice should be at the heart of every progressive's activism. LGBTQ friends deserve full personhood and protections. Torture is never OK. Black lives matter. Islam isn't a terrorist religion. No human being is illegal. There are hundreds of other statements: truths that should be accepted by all, and more thoughtfully considered by each of us.

Commit yourself to better understanding other points of view and developing empathy (see Action #10). Speak up and try to educate others about what you see happening. Standing up for others takes courage and smarts. Since you are both courageous and smart, the world is in luck! You will have many opportunities to speak up for justice. Sometimes that will mean raising your hand in class to point out a stereotype; sometimes it will mean telling a friend that a joke is unacceptable; and sometimes it will mean getting yourself out of a situation and somewhere safe to call home. Practice judging a situation before diving in potentially over your head. Remember to discuss these types of scenarios in your family meeting—see Action #3. (Still haven't had the family meeting? Schedule it today!)

May We Suggest ...

Using your voice when you see an injustice can sometimes be hard, especially when you're not yet in practice. The good news is it doesn't have to be some epic Hollywood monologue. All it often takes are three little words that make it clear you are not cool with what is happening: That's not okay.

It's a great sentence because it lets you choose what you want to emphasize, depending on how ticked off you are at that moment: That's NOT okay. THAT is not okay. (Or how we feel reading the paper each morning: THAT IS NOT OKAY.) You can even make it a more casual smackdown: Dude, that's not okay. Practice that phrase and put it in your pocket, and you will always have something easy to pull out in an ugly situation.

68. Resist ICE cold, ICE cruel policies

From the idiotic notion of a wall across our Southern border to the un-American detention centers and the ugly travel ban on Muslims, there is no denying there's a war on undocumented, immigrant, refugee, and marginalized people in this country. What some are calling "leadership" is really a brutish, lazy attack on people of color and the very ideals of this country's democracy. You may live seemingly far away from these issues, or you may be right on the front line. It doesn't matter. We need to say with one voice that we reject and resist these policies and toxic ideas. Call and write appropriately angry letters to your representatives who vote for this kind of nonsense (and thank-you messages to those who don't) and then turn a more gentle, loving eye to these ways to get involved:

- The National Immigrant Justice Center (www.immigrantjustice. org) has a list of active ICE facilities (mouseover *Issues* and click on *Immigration Detention & Enforcement* and scroll to the bottom of the page). Look for one near you, and figure out a way to help the people there.
- Write to thank a sanctuary city, community, organization, or congregation.
- Donate to organizations supplying legal assistance at detention centers, such as the Immigrant Defense Project (www. immigrantdefenseproject.org), the National Immigrant Justice Center (www.immigrantjustice.org), and the ACLU (click Issues and then Immigrants' Rights from www.aclu. org).
- Donate to organizations working for immigrants' rights, such as United We Dream (www.unitedwedream.org).
- If you are old enough, you can sign up through Community Initiatives for Visiting Immigrants in Confinement (www. endisolation.org) to visit detainees. They also offer other opportunities to get involved. Check them out!
- Help sponsor a refugee family or donate supplies to make them feel more welcome. You can ask at local mosques, churches, and temples to see if they have sponsored anyone who might need help. Or Google *refugee resettlement charity* and the nearest biggish city to find services to contact.

- Bring a meal to the volunteer attorney working in international airport terminals to assist immigrants entering the United States.

69. Protect our precious parks

So much for "This land is your land, this land is my land." With a stroke of his pen, the ruiner-in-chief signed an executive order that threatens some of our precious national parks and monuments. (He asked his Department of the Interior to review public lands and determine whether to remove protections on them. Why? It's fair to assume that the mining, logging, and oil industries are involved.)

The Bears Ears National Monument in southeastern Utah is especially vulnerable. President Obama had issued a proclamation adding an extra layer of protection to Bears Ears, by granting its management to five Tribes with ancestral ties to the area. Reversing Obama's proclamation and lifting the moratorium on mining in federal lands are worrisome signs of what's to come. Help honor and protect our shared national treasures. Stand up for environmental justice, and pay special attention to areas and issues that impact the most vulnerable people.

- Go to the Southern Utah Wilderness Alliance (suwa.org) and get involved in protecting Bears Ears.

- Check out the Hot Issues tab at the Wilderness Society (wilderness.org) for lots of important information concerning national parks and monuments and how to protect them.

- The National Parks Conservation Association (www.npca. org) works on issues from park funding and advocacy to threats from global warming and the energy sector.

- Senators Martin Heinrich and Lamar Alexander sponsored the bipartisan Every Kid Outdoors (EKO) Act in July 2017. If it has not passed by the time you read this, call your senators and ask them to support it. Passing the EKO would make into law President Obama's Every Kid in a Park initiative to provide free National Parks admission for fourth-graders and their families.

70. Criminal justice reform

By now we're all painfully aware that elections have consequences. As a country we—across party lines—had begun discussing the need for comprehensive criminal justice reform. But now rather than working toward a healthier, better, more civilized union, we're stuck fighting nonsense and stupidity from all angles. Now it's up to the organizations in the trenches to lead the way for the criminal justice reform that our country desperately needs. These groups need your support to resist the policies of this administration and keep inching forward toward real reform.

- Support the Sentencing Project (www.sentencingproject. org) any way you can. Donate, download their amazing fact sheets and raise awareness, go to Take Action and make some calls.... This is your one-stop shop to find a way to make a difference You can also connect to their partner organizations in your state: www.sentencingproject.org/ state-contacts.

- Watch *13th*, the powerful, painful, and important documentary by Ava DuVernay that directly links the Thirteenth Amendment, which made slavery illegal, and this country's epidemic of mass incarceration. (Please note that Common Sense Media has recommended this documentary for mature teens and up. Please do not watch it without talking to your adult first.)

- Join in the campaign at Campaign for Youth Justice (www. campaignforyouthjustice.org) to help raise the age of minors being treated as adults in the criminal justice system. The Family Resource Booklet has information and resources regarding every aspect of criminal justice reform; find it in the Take Action tab under Family Engagement.

71. Money + Politics = Seriously Shady

Oh, money. Where do we begin? How, why, when does a government raise money, spend money, waste money, save money, allocate money, and even print money? Who gets the money? Which projects deserve funding? What industries should be supported? Which are too big to fail or too small to care about, no matter how important or innovative their work? Keep in mind that one big bomb (that we should never, ever use) costs a billion dollars, but National Public Radio needs to justify its very existence every time a conservative comes to power. Oh, money. Where do we begin?

You can't really talk about change without understanding how to fund it or how to combat the money that's funneling in, actively working to *prevent* the change from ever happening. There are many decent people and many decent corporations out there doing good work and making good money. (Really! Google it.) And thankfully there are more and more of them. But for many people and corporations—please forgive the expression—money trumps all else.

When it comes to politics, this is just as true. Money (and power) trumps all else. *Boo!* The issues are too vast (and frankly too depressing to get into), so we'll leave it to these good organizations, sites, and ideas that are working hard to change the way money rules in this country:

- You can spend all day learning about money in politics in *Money in Politics A to Z* (moneyinpolitics.us). They call it their primer in pay-to-play politics, and they don't pull any punches. Also watch *PAY 2 PLAY: Democracy's High Stakes,* a documentary that examines how big donors give big money to politicians who turn around and reward the donors with tax cuts, government contracts, and deregulation. When you're done watching, click over to SaveOurElections.org for loads of ideas and articles about what you can do: www.saveourelections.org/money-in-politics or go to the site and click on the Money in Politics link.

- Remember OpenSecrets.org from Action #32? We told you there was more! Check out the Outside Spending section, which takes a look at the outside groups that spend a LOT of money to influence elections (almost $1.5 billion in the 2016 presidential race). Also don't miss the Dark Money section, which looks at groups that spend money but keep their donors "dark," meaning who that money is from is unnamed.

- Join the Stampede at www.stampstampede.org. Beloved Ben and Jerry's cofounder Ben Cohen started this organization that lets you physically stamp currency to protest big money in politics.

- Ask your Senators and everyone you know to get behind Campaign Finance Reform, specifically the Fair Elections Now Act that would completely change how U.S. Senate elections are financed. The Fair Elections Now Act would give matching funds, grants, and vouchers to qualified candidates to run campaigns on smaller-dollar contributions and not big-money donors.

72. The health care headache

Health care is complicated ... and confusing and upsetting and personal and scary in some ways. If you are reading this and know lots about accessing and paying for health care, chances are you or someone you love has been caught in the middle of those complications. And if you're a healthy, able-bodied young person, you might already be looking for the off-switch on this action because, *man*, is thinking about health care boring (and complicated and confusing and upsetting and personal and scary). But stick around because this mess has *gotta* be figured out, and every voice is needed! Even better: health care is one of those issues where there is plenty of common ground (don't let all of that D.C. finger-pointing and posturing fool you).

- Become a single-payer champion. Check out one of many, many single-payer advocacy groups. Single-payer isn't the answer to everything, but the more you understand and educate people on alternatives to the way the health care system works (or doesn't!), the more productive the conversation. Physicians for a National Health Program (www. pnhp.org) is a great place to start.

- Keep an eye on health care legislation. Countable (www. countable.us) offers nonpartisan summaries and reviews of pending legislation across all sorts of issues. Just type in "health care" (or pretty much any other topic you're interested in), and Countable will help you track what's happening.

- If you or someone in your family is ill and feels particularly vulnerable about the future of health care, consider writing out your personal story. Then send your story to your representatives (or deliver it in person—see Action #51). It may not bring results, but at least writing down what you're worried about organizes your thoughts and your voice is entered into the public record. Also be sure to keep your story handy: it will make a good letter to the editor (see Action #35) when health care is in the headlines again.

73. Black Lives Matter Matters

Black Lives Matter has become a lightning rod for people acting like it's something controversial to say, but we quite frankly don't see the big deal. Black lives DO matter. Full stop. How could that be controversial? BLACK LIVES DO MATTER. Don't let folks politicize it and turn it into something ugly. It's not about white. It's not about brown or blue or yellow or red or chartreuse. It's about being black and how that can be a dangerous way to be in this country. It's about letting yourself see that danger, and it's about understanding that it just plain sucks that anyone should be endangered or should feel endangered because their skin is black. And it's about seeing the value of black citizens and lives in the country and saying for all to hear that Black Lives Matter.

BLM is a reaction to the irrefutable fact that black people are stopped, searched, arrested, and killed more often by police than any other group and in numbers that should make every American take to the streets. This is not the kind of country you want to live in. It is not a black issue; it is an American issue.

If you meet someone who still struggles to understand why All Lives Matter is an inappropriate response to Black Lives Matter, there are any number of analogies to help explain it. Here's a common one: Everyone is hungry and sits down at the table. Everyone but Mark is given a plate of food. When Mark says he is hungry, the others say, "*Everyone* is hungry, Mark." Yes, everyone is hungry ("everyone matters"), but Mark is being denied the food. To talk about anyone else's hunger when Mark has no food is inappropriate, offensive, and ignores the point.

Here's what you can do:

- Go to Black Lives Matter (blacklivesmatter.com) and read up on the organization's platform. Go to How You Can Help to look up a chapter near you.
- Get involved with Campaign Zero's (www.join campaignzero. org) comprehensive plan to end police violence and improve community interactions.
- Listen to an interview with the founders of Black Lives Matter at www.ted.com (search Black Lives Matter).
- Don't shy away from talking about race. Teaching Tolerance (www.tolerance.org), an amazing resource provided by the good people at the Southern Poverty Law Center, provides

wonderful—free!—resources to schools and individuals. Read the *Let's Talk! Discussing Race, Racism & Other Difficult Topics with Students* pdf, and make sure your school has a copy, too. Find it at www.tolerance.org/magazine/publications/lets-talk, or by mousing over Magazines & Publications and clicking Publications.

74. Fight for LGBTQ rights and protections

The country has recently taken some pretty giant steps toward recognizing, protecting, and celebrating the LGBTQ community. But these glorious, amazing gains that celebrated how love is love is love is love are now being threatened. Regressives—a kinder word for narrow-minded homophobes and haters—have been made bold by this disgusting political climate and are fighting tooth and nail to deny legal protections and roll back gains such as marriage rights and support for transgender soldiers who put their lives on the line for this country. As this lousy president courts an increasingly smaller and meaner base, he seems only too happy to throw the LGBTQ under the bus to satisfy them.

It's time for those of us on the right side of history to start fighting back tooth and nail to protect what is right and just. Hate crimes and bullying directed at the LGBTQ community are on the rise again. This is *unacceptable*. Even talk, let alone action, directed at ending civil rights protections for LGBTQ peoples is *unacceptable*.

There are wonderful organizations resisting this ugliness. Support them, please!

- First, if you are LGBT or Q (or just a letter that doesn't like labels) and are without a safe, supportive community around you, run, don't walk, to the fabulous It Gets Better Project: www.itgetsbetter.org. Keep in mind that It Gets Better Project is not an overtly political organization, but it has been a lifeline for a generation of kids looking for validation, reassurance, and community.
- The Live Out Loud network offers a page loaded with opportunities to get involved. Go to www.liveoutloud.info/resources/lgbt-youth-organizations or mouseover Resources and click on LGBT Youth Organizations.
- If you don't think you know a transgender person, learn about their lives and realities. The National Center for Transgender Equality (www.transequality.org) is a tremendous site filled with all sorts of valuable information. Be sure to check out their About Transgender People tab!
- The Trans Lifeline is a hotline for transgender people, by transgender people: www.translifeline.org.

75. Be your body's advocate

Planned Parenthood provides crucial health services to women and girls all over this country but because everything—*EVERYTHING*—is politicized in this country, the organization is constantly in danger. Certain lawmakers and zealots want to legislate abortion and are willing—even determined—to sacrifice women and women's health in the process. Do not allow them to toss out women's self-determination and health. Women and girls: we deserve access to quality health care without judgment. We deserve access to real health information and advocacy. We deserve access to affordable birth control. And we deserve access to abortion if we need it. Men and boys: we deserve you being part of this fight with us, too. Join with us.

Get informed. Get involved. How? Here are two amazing places to get started. They've got your back.

- Advocates for Youth (www.advocatesforyouth.org) offers a Get Involved tab but also so much more, including a Policy & Advocacy section jammed with ways to work to change the policy landscape as well as ways to change the conversations going on around you.
- What can we possibly say about the glorious Advocates for Youth Amplify project (amplifyyourvoice.org)? Swoon. Run there right now.

76. Humanize gun control

Gun violence statistics are staggering and downright depressing. Every side of the gun debate is fraught with friction and controversy. Every effort at creating common sense gun regulation seems to be met with mistrust and misinformation, followed by seemingly looser restrictions. Throw in stand-your-ground laws, open carry, and a politically emboldened class of crazies (yeah, we said it!) and ... well, you've got your work cut out for you.

Our advice is to *arm* yourself (see what we did there?) with as much information as you can. Start by reading the Second Amendment and by learning some basic gun facts and statistics. Have a working understanding of the different kinds of firearms. Too often activists undermine their argument by using confusing and imprecise terms. Next, really reflect on guns in your area. Are they prevalent? Revered? Used for sport? Used for power? What are your local and state gun laws? Finally, read up on the National Rifle Association (the NRA). The NRA is a relatively small organization that casts an ENORMOUS shadow over legislators through well-aimed large donations and *very* vocal and well-planned advocacy.

The good news is studies show that even most gun owners support common sense gun legislation. But tread lightly when talking with gun owners. (Duh! They're armed!) Keep in mind that they are constantly being told that liberals are planning to take away their guns. Be the face of common sense. Humanize our "side" by being open to listening to their side and by patiently explaining what common sense gun legislation is *really* about. There is plenty of common ground here.

- Americans for Responsible Solutions was started by former congresswoman Gabby Giffords, who was shot while holding an outdoor meeting for constituents: americansforresponsiblesolutions.org
- Everytown for Gun Safety (everytown.org) offers a thriving Act section to get you started as well as a clearly organized Learn section on everything from the gun lobby to domestic violence to background checks.
- The Law Center to Prevent Gun Violence (smartgunlaws. org) offers detailed descriptions of each state's gun laws as well as a downloadable factsheet comparing that state's laws to the other states. Go to Gun Laws and select State Laws to find a list of all 50 states plus the District of Columbia.

77. Fight for economic justice

Issues of economic justice affect nearly everything and every group. Poverty; unfair wages; lack of suitable job opportunities; divestment; housing costs; crumbling consumer, environmental, and worker protections; and increasing efforts to dismantle the public safety net all disproportionately affect communities of color and the elderly, but no one is immune. The rich get richer. The poor get poorer. This is waaaaay truer today than it has ever been before. While we like to say that this country was founded on pluck and hard work, those qualities won't get you far anymore.

Did you know that a 2017 study by the National Low Income Housing Coalition found that people making the federal minimum wage of $7.25 per hour would need to work 117 hours per week to afford a two-bedroom home renting at fair market value? The study also found that there are only 12 counties in the entire country where a full-time minimum-wage worker could actually afford to rent a one-bedroom home. This struggle might be your own reality, or it might be shocking news to you. Either way, become involved and fight for fair wages and economic practices.

- See Actions #105 and #106 for advice on how to be a better consumer.
- Champion affordable housing! Visit the National Low Income Housing Coalition website (nlihc.org), which features a thriving Take Action section as well as a Get Involved section that lists affordable-housing organizations in almost every state. (If your state is one of the few without an organization listed, write the national organizer for your area and see what you can do to help put some pressure out there to get one created.)
- United for a Fair Economy (www.faireconomy.org) has a zillion helpful resources and activities, but be sure to check out the Training Guides (under Resources) if you *really* want to inform yourself about the economy and the sources of its inequalities.
- If it is offered, take an Econ class! Your understanding of larger fiscal issues and your own personal money sense are super

important. If you want to supplement your education, maybe start an Economics Club and work through these awesome lesson plans generously shared by Teaching Economics as if People Mattered: www.teachingeconomics.org.

78. Squash the science debate

A small segment of people—ones who are anti-science and gleefully, joyously, ridiculously anti-intellectual (?!?!!)—are attempting to take down science. SCIENCE, of all things! Ummm, yeah: isn't science the topic so important that it's taught in freakin' school? While it's cool and all that the Internet has given every person a chance to be heard, it's not cool that people now seem to think that a Google search makes them more of an expert than the scientific community. Let's give that a big, fat NO, folks! Each moment we pause to listen to someone make a pronouncement like, [insert dumb voice here] *if we really came from apes there wouldn't be apes still around*, we get distracted from the task at hand. Stop debating the deniers. Instead, get involved. You're going to be the ones who use science to answer the world's challenges. Study, relish, and celebrate science!

• Pay attention in science class. Science is a challenging subject, but these are challenging times (and believe it or not, you'll pull those science concepts out in conversations the rest of your life). Ask questions, be curious, wonder!

- Latinx and Indigenous folks interested in science should join SACNAS (the Society for Advancement of Chicanos/ Hispanics and Native Americans in Science) at sacnas.org and help diversify the field and spread the message.
- Girls Who Code (girlswhocode.com) runs programs all over the world to teach girls coding in an effort to close up the worrisome gender gap in tech careers.
- Does your school have a STEAM (Science, Technology, Engineering, Art, and Math) club? Join or talk to a science teacher about starting one.
- Be sure to support local science (see Action #97) by supporting any nearby science museums.
- Google "Masters for Data Science Ultimate STEM Guide for Kids." You won't believe how many cool things you'll find to explore!
- The Union of Concerned Scientists (www.ucsusa.org) runs several advocacy campaigns. Check out its Take Action section.

79. Fight for the planet

As you already know, climate change is real—and *really* serious. If this isn't an issue that gets your blood boiling, it should be. Many talented thinkers are working hard to slow the demise of our planet and come up with real, sustainable solutions (don't believe us? look at the very long—but still incomplete—list of groups to check out below!). But the climate deniers (and climate we-don't-care-one-single-bit-ers) have been emboldened by this greedy buffoon of a privileged leader. (That's not to mention the industry opportunists who don't bat an eyelash when choosing profit over doing the right thing.) We must stand strong against these selfish ignoramuses who will blissfully whistle as they spread destruction and environmental injustice. They will try to dismantle regulations, privatize what once was protected, and do anything they can to "win." Well, we don't define winning this way, and you don't need to either. Stand up and resist!

- SustainUS (sustainus.org) is just for you, young resistance members. The group holds campaigns to create delegations of youths to send to conferences. Follow its Twitter feed: @SustainUS.
- Also don't miss the International Youth Climate Movement (youthclimatemovement.wordpress.com or follow @IYCM).
- There are so many good people and organizations working on this issue. Here's just a handful: the Peoples Climate Movement (peoplesclimate.org), 350 (350.org), and Greenpeace Greenwire (greenwire.greenpeace.org/usa/en/).
- Environmentalists of faith should check out Interfaith Power & Light (www.interfaithpowerandlight.org), which works to be "faithful stewards of Creation."
- The League of Conservation Voters can help you find a group working in your state: www.lcv.org/state-affiliates.

- The United States may have pulled out of the Paris Climate Agreement, but many cities, counties, colleges, and businesses (even big oil companies!) still vow to uphold the proposed standards of the agreement. Study the amazing list at We Are Still In (www.wearestillin.com). Write postcards of support to companies (see Action #47) and urge your county to sign on.

- Watch these documentaries: *An Inconvenient Truth* (both 1 and 2), *True Cost*, and *Who Killed the Electric Car?* Host a documentary night to spread the message! (See Action #88 for help.)

- Make a plan to reduce your family's carbon footprint. Find some terrific resources at carbonfund.org. Challenge a friend or another family to a reduction competition and share ideas and triumphs.

80. Net Neutrality

It's got to be hard to wrap your head around the fact that there was a time—not all that long ago—when people looked up things in encyclopedias and not on their smartphones. Oh, the humanity! We shouldn't joke: we love our devices and Internet as much as you do. Sort of. While many of us old'uns use the Internet as a faster, lighter, portable encyclopedia, your generation's very imagination is linked to the possibilities of the giant world wide web. *You* will best wrestle with the ethics and challenges of so much free speech, and *you* will best understand and utilize its potential. That is, if it remains free flowing.

In 2015, the Federal Communications Commission (FCC) deemed the Internet a public utility, much like water or energy. In doing so, it made it impossible for Internet providers (despite their many attempts) to speed up or slow down Internet sites in exchange for money. But thanks to the Internet's public utility status, all its sites theoretically load equally quickly and are therefore equally available. Without that status, we'd probably only see sites that paid money to the Internet providers. It's good regulation. It keeps the Internet innovative and *neutral*. That's net neutrality, people.

This president doesn't like regulations. He doesn't like regulations to protect water or sacred land or people's access to the ballot box, and he doesn't give one byte about keeping the Internet neutral. He appointed a new head to the FCC who has begun the process of deregulating the Internet and has the nerve to call it "restoring Internet freedom." *GAG!* Protecting net neutrality is really important! Here's how to help:

- Find out where your representatives stand at www.battleforthenet. com and make phone calls or tweets thanking them for or asking them to support net neutral legislation.
- Writing a letter to the FCC in support of net neutrality couldn't be easier. Dearfcc.org from the Electronic Frontier Foundation provides the template with space to write a paragraph about what the Internet means to you.
- People have heard about net neutrality but might not understand what it means or how it would affect them.

Inform yourself, then help spread the word: the Electronic Frontier Foundation (www.eff.org), Fight for the Future (www.fightforthefuture.org), and the Center for Media Justice (centerformediajustice.org) are good places to start. You'll find ideas on how to raise awareness of the issues you care about in the next chapter.

81. Protect the vote

We'd like to say there's absolutely nothing more un-American than voter suppression, but that's not entirely true. People and parties have used voter suppression tactics throughout our history, so maybe trying to win by keeping people from voting IS American. But it shouldn't be. And it shouldn't be tolerated. Ever! It's a lesson politicians should have learned in preschool: cheating isn't winning.

The cheaters will try to convince you of widespread voter fraud. It is not true. Massive purges to the voter rolls, bogus voter ID laws, closing polling places, and shortening early voting times are nothing but direct attacks on democracy—especially on people of color, disabled people, and the elderly. Know your stuff. Push back. Shame the cheaters. For more ways to get involved, visit/support/ love these wonderful organizations:

- The ACLU provides a terrific overview of voter issues at www.aclu.org/issues/voting-rights (or go to Voting Rights listed under Issues). For more on the ACLU, see Action #102.

- Learn about ranked-choice voting (you can even download an activist toolkit) at the nonpartisan FairVote (fairvote. org).
- Rock the Vote (rockthevote.com) has been working since 1990 to get young people to understand their political power. The group has registered millions of new voters. Sign up for action alerts and election reminders.
- Lastly, make a promise. Once you are allowed to vote, vow to *never* miss an election!

82. Give peace your commitment

Imagine a world free of fear and war and violence. Is it attainable? Probably not. Should that stop you from working toward peace and disarmament? No. Way. You are the future. You are the future leaders. You are the future business people. You are the future negotiators and caregivers and changemakers. (#iamthefuture) You get to define what winning means, what success looks like, and how you choose to live. Make the pledge: be peaceful. Dedicate your talents to peace. Dream it, then work toward living it.

- Observe and promote International Peace Day on September 21. Peace One Day (peaceoneday.org) has wonderful activities to organize in your community in the Get Involved section. (The rest of that site is inspiring as well!)

- Head over to Don't Bank on the Bomb (www.dontbankonthebomb. com) to learn about the financial institutions that invest in the production and modernization of nuclear weapons. Send them a postcard stating that you won't be choosing a bank that actively profits off of nuclear weapons.

- The more we understand and connect to other people and cultures (see Actions #22 and #12), the more we humanize each other, making the idea of waging war on people with similar (and different!) dreams and hopes less and less palatable. There are some pretty fancy (read: pricey!) organizations that send teens across the globe to work and live among other cultures. If money isn't an obstacle, absolutely consider it. The index of opportunities at Global Leadership Adventures (www.experiencegla.com) is enough to make any advocate swoon. (You'll find plenty of low-cost ideas for expanding your worldview in Chapter 2.)

83. Take to the streets

Of course, the grandmama of all activism is the political march— a time-honored, time-proven tradition. When the opportunity presents itself in your area, get out there and march (find some at Resistance Near Me, resistancenearme.org, and at Resistance Calendar, www.resistancecalendar.org). Resisting megalomaniac tyrants, changing the world, restoring faith in democracy … it's going to be a slow slog. By adding yourself to the numbers of people willing to spill out into the street for a better world, you signal that you aren't worried about how long it's going to take, that you're vigilant and willing to work. As an added bonus the experience of collective resistance is affirming and energizing and powerful. March if you can.* Bring friends and families if you can. Relish your sore feet and hoarse voice—you've done good.

* Sadly, we need to include one caveat: Talk to your adults before marching. Emotions are running hot in our country: flare-ups of violence at protests are terribly disheartening and all too real. Do march if you can and are allowed but **be safe**. Keep #iamthefuture in mind and remember that we *need* all of you to be *in* that future.

PART THREE

FROM ACTIVIST TO ADVOCATE

• • •

"To the young folks of all ethnicities I say #staywoke not as a catchphrase but as a lifestyle. Most of the things that are killing us are in our minds and our daily routines."

—DICK GREGORY,
ACTIVIST AND COMEDIAN

CHAPTER SEVEN

Raising Awareness

Actions to Spread Your Message

● ● ●

"Put the message in the box
Put the box into the car.
Drive the car around the world
Until you get heard."

—KARL WALLINGER,
WORLD PARTY, "PUT THE MESSAGE IN THE BOX"

Dear Advocate,

This isn't normal. You may have heard that a lot lately. There are days when I mutter it all day long, as if by saying *This isn't normal*, I can fend off the orange menace from destroying the very ideals of this country ... along with the physical land, soul, and institutions as well. If we wear sparkly shoes, click our heels, and say it three times, will we wake from this political nightmare? *This isn't normal. This isn't normal. This isn't....*

STOP! We *aren't* political dreamers! We are advocates, damnit! We don't stand slack-jawed in the middle of our lives, dumbfounded. We don't rely on mantras and wishful thinking!

We mobilize. We work. We act. And we raise awareness!

In the daily swirl of the circus that this administration has become, we keep our wits about us and cut through the constant din of chaos and distraction to help people stay focused on the task at hand, on the lives hanging in the balance, and on the causes and organizations we feel most passionate about.

We're not in Kansas anymore,

Joanna

P.S. Do people even watch *The Wizard of Oz* anymore? If you didn't get any of the above references, roll your eyes, then jump right into the chapter. You don't need any fancy introductions.

84. Lend your social media savvy

Are you a savvy social media type with a passion for a certain cause? Find a local organization you care about and ask if it needs help with its social media. It might already have a social media presence, in which case you could ask if you can help out with that. Or—even more exciting—it might have no or not much of a social media voice, in which case you could get to craft their whole "brand," keeping in mind their audience and what kind of information they need to get out there. Either way, the organization will likely be delighted to have some skilled help (and it will look fantastic on your résumé).

85. Start a salon? *Oui!*

In eighteenth-century France, people came together in small, organized groups to talk about the political and social issues of the day. They met in people's living rooms, or *salons*. Salons moved to coffeeshops and across the Atlantic to this country where intellectuals, artists, and dreamers came together to discuss and strategize. Consider bringing the salon back. Identify a cause or an issue to discuss, and invite thoughtful friends to your living room, coffeehouse, or pretty park and talk, share, and imagine together. (If you think your friends might find it a little strange to be invited to an intellectual exchange, how about invite them for cookies? Sugar is always an excellent motivator!)

Oh, we know what you're thinking. *Group text!* We're not here to throw shade at your digital lives, but you might consider meeting in real life for this. Meeting IRL still has its place. When humans come together with purpose and common intentions, there's an energy ... even when unplugged.

86. Book it to help your cause

Have you read a book on an issue you'd like others to know about? Write up a short review (just a paragraph or two) of the book on why you think it's worthwhile reading. (Need book ideas? See Action #15.) Provide a list of other books that deal with the topic and throw in some high-quality facts (check them first!—see Action #28), websites, or movies that deal with the same issue. Share your work with friends and family. Also send your write-up to your local librarian friend (see Action #5) to see if the library has any interest in including it in their newsletter. You could also propose that the library challenge others to work on their own curated lists and create a display about all kinds of topics that are near and dear to people in your community.

87. Curate for the cause

If you prefer art over books, consider curating an art exhibit that deals with an issue dear to your heart. It could be a solo show, or you can invite creative kids (adults, too, if you'd like) to explore, for example, the separation of church and state through their art. Find a place to display it. It doesn't have to be on a lighted white wall; it could be on the grass of someone's backyard, a meeting room in the library, or your front stoop.

A little note about art: art, especially, can be provocative, and what is provocative is subjective—it's different for everybody. Indeed, many would argue that art is supposed to be provocative. If art depicts something that is difficult to talk about, it can be a triumph in terms of starting the discussion. It can also mean that it might be offensive to someone else. Make some decisions with your adults about what, if any, guidelines you'd like to establish for your show. If you're hoping for a larger audience, be sure to send out a news release (see Action #40) to help you advertise the event. (And remember: BE SURE TO TALK TO YOUR FAMILY before inviting a larger audience!)

88. Host a documentary night

Many fab documentaries take on the concerns of the world. Let them do the heavy lifting of helping you to get the word out about what concerns you the most. Host a documentary night where you provide the popcorn, and the movie provides the message.

If you're worried that a whole movie will be too long for your audience, instead trying using a TED talk or two on the topic you care about and cap it off with a fun movie of your choice. (You might even be able to marry the two—like a TED talk about climate change and a showing of cheesy global-warming disaster film "The Day After Tomorrow" or Pixar classic "WALL-E.")

What Is a TED Talk?

You might have seen a TED Talk in school at some point. TED Talks (ted.com) are short lectures about all kinds of interesting and powerful topics where experts share their knowledge about just about anything (TED used to stand for Technology, Entertainment and Design, but topics are no longer limited to that). Not sure where to start? Go to Watch and then Playlists, and look for Talks by Brilliant Kids and Teens. Tune in and prepare to be dazzled, enlightened, and possibly even woke.

89. Get out the vote

You may not be old enough to vote, but that shouldn't stop you from reminding others to take voting very seriously (see Action #81). Write letters (both old-fashioned paper ones and emails) to your older friends and neighbors about the importance of voting—that it is the most important right and privilege that democracy provides its citizens. You don't have to ask people to vote for anyone specific, just ask them to engage. (This would be a great topic for a letter to the editor—see Action #35.)

Be sure your letters includes information on registering to vote (not all adults are registered) and also about early voting (which varies from state to state so be careful if you are writing anyone far away).

90. Speak out

Sometimes speaking out is as easy as looking right outside your front door. See if you can get your message out to a wider audience through groups you are already involved in. Like if you're involved in a business club at school, go to PolicyLink (www.policylink. org)—a group that advocates real-world, practical solutions to problems of equity—and read up on equitable development practices. Find the Equity Development Toolkit in the Equity Tools area. The Economic Opportunity section showcases eight tested methods for being sure economic development includes *all* citizens.

Or if you regularly attend a faith institution, see if you can get it involved in the fight to protect the environment. How about reading and writing a brief book review of *Green Mama* by pastor Tracey Bianchi and submitting it to your church bulletin? Bianchi provides practical suggestions for caring for the environment within a broader framework of caring and respecting God's creation. Or read *God in the Wilderness: Rediscovering the Spirituality of the Great Outdoors with the Adventure Rabbi* by Jamie S. Korngold, take in her lessons on reawakening your inner spirituality and sense of purpose, and share your new viewpoint with others in your synagogue. Or look up *Green Deen: What Islam Teaches about Protecting the Planet* by Ibrahim Abdul-Matin and see how he traces Islam's historic dedication to being stewards of the earth. Put a review of it up on the bulletin board at your mosque.

91. Show some drive

Connecting your groups with causes (see the previous Action—#90—to get yourself started with that) makes for effective advocacy. You not only reach out to a larger audience and spread your message that way, but you also work to build bridges among people—even, maybe, among those who might not think they have much in common. Like you may not share the same political leanings with the people who live in your building or larger community, but you can build some trust and respect amongst your neighbors by organizing a shoe drive for Souls4Souls (soles4souls. org). This might lead you into a conversation about, say, economic injustice in the world and in this country (see Action #34 for help with talking with people with other viewpoints). And once you open that door in your neighbor's mind and help make the link between charity and the root causes of the need for that charity, well, who knows?

92. Give gifts for the greater good

Every time you celebrate someone's birthday, challenge yourself to really *give* in their honor. Donate time or money to a cause that is important to the person celebrating. Even if you don't share each other's progressive perspective, use the gift as an opportunity to think and give creatively. Pick a cause or organization you both would be happy to support. Maybe a tee from vividroots.com that donates 20% of their profits to implement clean water systems in developing countries would be a good fit!

If you do share the same progressive spirit, the sky's the limit in terms of opportunities, even when your budget isn't. Give a personalized list of the person's representatives (local, state, and national) including contact information in their card. Also add a little advice on how quick and easy the script to call can look (see Action #48). You could also do their homework by collecting articles on a given cause (include ways for them to get involved), curate a fascinating list of TED Talks, or create a playlist of modern world music. Regardless, make giving for good your *thing*!

93. Wear your heart on your sleeve ... literally

Buy or, better yet, design a T-shirt (or button or piece of jewelry) that makes a statement about something you care about. There are many issue T-shirts out there: some you can buy to raise money for an organization, and some you can make at the kitchen table with a permanent marker. Wearable statements can draw lots of attention at school, so your best bet is to choose a quote or message that inspires, not divides. No matter the setting, challenge yourself to keep it positive. (But if you want to make yourself an angry, nasty one to wear to bed, we would totally support that and might even ask you to make us one. Some news days just call for nightwear that screams and curses and vents.)

94. Chalk the walk

You'll need to borrow your little brother's sidewalk chalk for this one. Do you live in an area with sidewalks and decent foot traffic? If so, give people strolling by something to think about. Leave a colorful reminder for an important meeting or event, a thank you to an organization doing good work for the community, an inspirational quote such as "You really can change the world if you care enough." —Marian Wright Edelman, or a statistic on climate change. A note: when you take your activism to public places, it's important to keep the message positive and upbeat. People are more likely to think openly about an idea when they're not feeling defensive about their own position.

Go the Extra Step

Chalking the walk would be a great action around Election Day. You don't have to post anything political—simply a reminder for one and all that voting is an important part of democracy and that everyone should vote. Remind people the dates that early voting starts and ends (if you have it in your area), and also post the date of Election Day as well. (And don't forget spring and non-presidential elections as well! If 2016 taught us anything it's that **ALL** elections are important.)

95. Talk, speak, converse, rap, gab ...

The best way to raise awareness is to talk about what you're interested in, what you're worried about, and how you are helping. Whatever you're doing to help this country live up to its ideals ...

well, we give you permission to brag about it. (And if someone asks to get involved in what you're doing—SMILE! You've not only raised awareness, you've inspired an activist! Kudos to you, young resistance member.)

CHAPTER EIGHT

Living with Intention

Actions to Live Your Values

• • •

"Compassion must be translated into action."

—NATASHA MAYERS,

ARTIST, EDUCATOR, AND ACTIVIST

Dearest Reader of Intention,

Oh how very much I wish I could promise you that your hard work will reap instant, noticeable rewards and that your activist efforts will make a measureable difference. It very well may. (In which case, awesome! Enjoy it! You've earned it.)

But the hard truth is that you may not see instant results. You may talk yourself blue in the face and still have everyone else in your household refuse to recycle. Or you may rave in disgust when you see yet another bunch of women objectified in a music video—but the objectifying video won't stop just because you've schooled your inner circle on its horrors. And you may boycott a business for years and years because its values are drastically different than your own, and yet that business is *still* around. (WTF! Really?!)

Yeah. Been there, done that. Proud to still be doing that, in fact. Why am I still at it after all these years and all these tears? Because you and I, my friend, are people of intention. We live by our values not because it looks good on social media or because it's bringing about the change we want but because we know it is the right thing to do and the right way to be—the *only* way, in fact, to truly live.

So embrace your intentions not for what they will do but for how they will enrich your life. Stand proud in your beliefs. Keep fighting the good fight and living thoughtfully. Whether it's in the way you spend your money, the way you live your life, or the way you talk, be the type of person who does it with intention.

Still boycotting those damned chicken sandwiches. Always.

Kerri

96. Lend a hand

Volunteer! To give of your valuable time not only provides an organization with help, but it shows that you value what the group stands for. Volunteer for a group in your community that is working to make a difference. (Don't forget to check out your religious institution—they're often working hard on local issues.)

Post volunteering photos and updates to help others see how great it feels to volunteer and to help spread the word about the good these groups are doing. Be sure to include any specific donation needs the organization has and information on how to give.

97. Show science some luv

Become a member of your local science museum or zoo. Can't afford it? Write to find out the minimum age to volunteer and give your support through donated time. Still too young? Email the director a letter explaining your support for science and asking what you can do to help her spread the message.

May We Suggest ...

If it's too much money to join a museum, look around the website and see if you can find any free days. (Museums sometimes offer certain days where no admission is charged.) Visit on one of those days, and be sure to post pictures from the trip and public shout-outs to how important science is for keeping us all safe and healthy and progressing toward a wonderful future.

98. Analyze the lyrics

You know those lyrics that you are screaming along with (or are just screaming along with in your head)? Rock, pop, rap, and country music historically have some pretty horrid messages mixed in the lyrics, but we don't even think about them as we're merrily singing along. Next time you're listening to some music, stop and listen to the words. For example, all of those rude words about women (you know the ones). Yeah, those aren't OK, and we know that—so why do we sing along and buy those songs? That song that talks about how a woman says "she won't" but the singer knows he'll still get at her? Ummm, yeah—that's sexual violence set to a catchy beat.

Especially think about songs that mention women of color—black women and Asian women particularly—because they are often particularly offensive and make it seem like those women only exist to be men's playthings. It's gross, offensive, and untrue, and it's time to stop buying it (pun intended).

We're not saying you have to stop listening (we wish we could say that we always think about it ourselves), but we are saying that we should all be conscious consumers of our culture—that we should think about what's going into our head and decide if that is OK with us or not. So listen up, and make a choice. (And don't hesitate to point it out to friends, and help them start to see the pattern, too.)

99. Watch and listen alone, process together

More than ever, people are listening to songs alone through their earbuds or watching TV and movies alone on different devices. What does this mean for how much the media messages translate straight into our brain's subconscious? No one really knows, but it is something that we should all be thinking about and be aware of. If what we are watching has an outright ugly message or a *well-hidden* ugly message, it might be becoming part of the way we think whether we want it to or not. Try talking about media with your friends. Consider starting a club. Discuss not just whether you liked the movie/song/show but about the message behind it. Get it out in the open. It definitely can't hurt to have it out there where you all can see it!

If you're not sure where to start with analyzing the media, visit the Critical Media Project (www.criticalmediaproject.org) to read up on the topic. While there, do *not* miss the Useful Links page at www.criticalmediaproject.org/resources/useful-links/ (or mouseover Resources and click on Useful Links).

100. Mind your language

Ah, the media. How it loves to kick around women and treat them as objects of sexual use and abuse (see Action #98), as objects of ridicule, as objects of disgust and scorn, as targets of violence. Basically any way the media can debase women, it has done so.

Let's not help them out in that campaign to make women one-dimensional, shall we? It can feel innocent to tell a friend to stop "acting like a girl," but our words are powerful. And don't get us started on that rude word—let's call that word "kitty"—that our slang culture likes to use to mean someone acting wimpy: "Come on, you kitty! Get out there."

Live your feminism with intention, and don't use hateful female-centered words to show powerlessness. The English language is vast and colorful and lovely, so really and truly, we don't need to use terms about women as insults anymore. (And don't forget the old trick from Action #67 on how to speak up when you hear insulting things in the conversations around you.)

101. Stop the fakers

Pressure corporations to stop advertising on alt-right sites loaded with fake news. (Remember, fake news is "news" purposefully created to mislead and manipulate. See Action #28 for more.) Did you know that some pretty big corporations give advertising money to groups that pretend to be newsgroups? These groups can have some pretty disgusting beliefs—like that only white people should have any power. (Did anyone else just puke a little in their mouth?) Pressure the companies that give these sites money by writing them and telling them that you and your family are not buying their products anymore until they stop advertising there. And then spread the word. Grow the boycott. (For more on boycotts, see Action #108.) Check the Sleeping Giants Facebook page (www.facebook.com/slpnggiants) and Twitter account (@slpng_giants) to find out what companies you should write to complain.

Go the Extra Step

Help to spread the word about boycotting the companies who advertise on these disgusto sites. Create a pamphlet (including the Sleeping Giants info would probably be a good idea), and leave several of them in visible places around your community—maybe the public library, the community center, the recreation center, the bus stop, and so on.

102. Carry your ideals with pride

Way, way, WAY back in 1988 (the year this writer cast a vote in her first presidential election) there was a lot of talk of being a "card-carrying member of the ACLU." Then-Vice President Bush (the first President Bush, the father—not the one that we thought would go down as this country's worst president but has since been elevated to an *OMG-I-wish-he-were-still-my-president-instead* status) lashed out at his competitor with that "insult" (?!) of being a "card-carrying member of the American Civil Liberties Union." Jeez, *soooo* insulting to be accused of being a member of an organization defending anyone's right to free speech (among many other things).

No matter who you are or what you're saying, the ACLU has your back. There is no other organization in this country that will work so hard to support and defend the rights afforded to you by the Constitution. Turn to its site as a reference guide or even as a source of comfort; they are doing much of the heavy-hitting resisting these days, under this new epically, historically, atrociously *worst* president. Sign up for their news alerts, and—if you are able—become a member! Carry that card proudly, young resistance member.

In fact, carry all your cards proudly. (Join many organizations if you can afford it!) Be proud of who you are and what you stand for. There will be people who will question you, dissuade you, disagree with you, and sometimes even mock you for your ideals. Carry your ideals proudly. You are learning to be an advocate. And you're poised to save the world!

103. Give 'em shelter

Calling all animal and nature lovers! Imagine if everyone could commit to turning their tiny corner of the world into a sanctuary for birds, butterflies, and other local wildlife. Awesome, right?! The National Wildlife Federation (www.nwf.org) would love to help. Its program Garden for Wildlife (www.nwf.org/Garden-For-Wildlife/Create.aspx, or find it under How to Help) was created in 1973 to educate people on the importance of protecting wildlife habitats through connecting people to nature right where they live. The organization walks you through the process of creating a sustainable habitat. Once you've gone through the steps, you can even certify your habitat through them. Creating a safe space for wildlife is easier than you think. (If you don't have access to a green space directly where you live, this would be a great action to propose for your synagogue, school, or local park.)

104. There's an app for that

Sometimes living with intention gets difficult. You're *trying* to pay attention. You're *trying* to do your part. You're *trying* to stay involved and engaged and appropriately angry. But life gets busy, and obligations to friends and family and work and/or school can get in the way. When you feel your intentions to be part of the resistance start to slip, turn to technology. Several apps and e-mail and text lists work to make it easy to stay politically active in these times. Daily Action (dailyaction.org) will text you a single action each day. Easy-peasy-lemon squeezy. (Texting rates apply, so be sure you're OK to get them.) My Civic Workout (www.mycivicworkout.com) uses old-fashioned email to keep you informed and is designed to inspire (and continue to motivate) new activists. (Plus it features the kick-butt tagline: "Your heart is a muscle the size of your fist. Keep loving, keep fighting.") The 65 (thesixtyfive.org) gives a weekly action and script and also has an awesome tagline: "We are the 65, and we're his problem now." (We resistance members are so clever!) Subscribe to Do a Thing by Shannon & Jane (tinyletter.com/doathing) to get a dose of smartaleckery and a concrete action in your email inbox. And last, but not least, 5 Calls (5calls.org) is an app that gives you five daily calls to make.

105. Put your money where your mouth is

How we spend our money is a big part of living intentionally—duh, this is America, after all. It's not necessarily something we think about all the time, but every single dollar we spend has a message attached: "I support you, Business Do-Right, and am OK with what you stand for."

Reward businesses and corporations that share your message or values by giving them your business. Think about your activist passions (go back to your message in Action #8), think about where you shop most, and then do some heavy researching online (watch for fake info—see Action #28) to find out how they intersect. Does the clothing store you shop at stand for your values? What about your makeup? Your hair products? (You can check out the Buycott app, www.buycott.com, to easily check out any products you use.)

Some heroic businesses have also taken possibly commercially risky steps in standing against this repulsive President and his repulsive messages. These companies need our thanks, our support, and our moola. Let them know that standing up to hate was worth the risk.

Also give some social media love (and good old-fashioned snail mail shoutouts) to those companies that support your ideals. Conservatives are *very* vocal when they disagree with a company's stance; we must openly match that level to help companies understand that they have our support.

106. *Don't* spend where your heart *isn't*

Where you choose to *not* spend your money is as powerful as where you do show your dollarly love. Sometimes you will have clear choices in where you spend your money (see Action #105), but often—alas—you won't. Does a national fast food chain have a loathsome stance toward LGBTQ people? Easy enough to know not to spend money there. What if it turns out that your wonderful new no-animal-testing shampoo company cooperates with ICE to round up undocumented workers? Do you keep buying the no-animal-testing shampoo even when you know that your money also supports ICE? That's a stickier decision to make, but it's a mental debate worth having so that any choices you make are being done with intention.

A decision to spend your money a certain way probably won't change the world (that fast food chain probably won't notice when you alone stop eating its fried chicken sandwiches), but the act of making these kinds of intentional decisions will change *your* world. You deciding how *you* want to spend your money and what kinds of businesses you want to support will empower you to live by your principles. (For ways to group up with like-minded consumers to hold a boycott, read on to Action #108.)

107. Be a green consumer

Being a green consumer is a classic way to spend your money intentionally—spending money where your values are supported and not spending money where they aren't. Become a green consumer today because it's the right thing to do and because it's a good way to say with intention that you know #iamthefuture. Live as softly as you can on the earth. Here are some ideas on easy changes to start yourself off:

- *Paying attention to packaging.* Buying local not only helps support local businesses but reduces the packaging and fuel of shipping.
- *Skip straws.* Traditional straws are non-biodegradable, single-use items, adding up to a disaster for our planet. Offer to make a sign for your favorite fast-food counter or restaurant explaining why skipping straws helps to eliminate trash for the waste stream. (Bonus incentive for the restaurant: they will save money on straws!)
- *Push fast fashion off the runway.* Those trendy and cheaply made fashions have a huge price tag for the planet when the worn or "out-of-fast-fashion" items are thrown away.
- *Shop second hand.* Go to thrift stores or resale shops when you are redoing your room or looking for a new outfit. You will find amazing choices at a fraction of the cost (with the bonus adventure of the thrill of the hunt!).
- *Pay a little more.* Companies often cut corners and outsource, or *ugly*source, in the name of profits. Reward businesses that ethically source and produce goods by being willing to pay a little more for them.

- *Encourage friends to follow your lead.* Speak out on why you are making your choices. Friends might not immediately mimic you, but you may plant a seed for their future actions.

108. Boycotts

OK, so here's the real deal on boycotts: it probably won't work. But knowing that doesn't mean you shouldn't do it. Standing up for your values is a reward of its own. Look, living with intention can be hard in this American culture, and when you finally, boldly take a stance—such as with a boycott—it's wildly satisfying.

A boycott—a concentrated, intentional effort to stop spending money with a certain business or company to express displeasure—is a time-honored activism tool. When you make a decision on your own, it's a statement. When it's you and several thousand of your closest friends who stop buying as a way to pressure a company, it's a thing of beauty.

To start a boycott, first do some heavy research to be sure you have all of your facts and figures about the company or product correct. (Trying calling or Tweeting the company's public relations department to confirm your findings.) Also reach out to the company to explain your boycott and the changes you hope to see, and then start spreading the word far and wide that others should boycott as well. (If you want to join an existing boycott, Google "list of progressive boycotts" to find loads of good info.)

If you'd like to aim your boycott at the President, there are a few Boycott Trump apps to check out and delight you. And if you really want to try to boycott *all* things to do with the grabber-in-chief, go to #grabyourwallet (grabyourwallet.org) to find out what stores and businesses support him, his companies, or his campaigns.

109. Make some noise

If you are absolutely furious about something a business or an organization has done and a boycott (Action #108) just doesn't feel like the right move, don't feel powerless! You are a person of intention who understands that your voice matters. Use that glorious, powerful, beautiful voice with intent. Work together with lots of friends to make your voices heard. Create a hashtag for your campaign—#CorporationXmuststop, for example—and get the hashtag trending (see Action #36). (And then double-up your message to traditional media by sending a letter to the editor, Action #35, explaining how you were so angry about this that you started an online campaign to change the policy. Even if you don't send a letter to the editor, be sure to @ a few local reporters in your Twitter campaign; they might be inspired to write a story.)

Your campaign doesn't have to be about something negative. Use your voice to harness the power of good news as well. You can also

Tweet thank-yous for policies or viewpoints or stances that you love. (And be sure to include the media on this positive campaign as well.)

110. Big impacts on small businesses

A last word on the idea of using your money to live intentionally: don't forget to consider local businesses when you are deciding where to spend (or not spend!) your money. Before you go to a local business think about its values: Do you like them? Do they take a role in the community and/or support the schools? Do they promote a lifestyle that you respect? Is it owned by a person—such as a woman or a person of color—that you want to support being represented in the business world?

Sometimes supporting a local business and what it stands for may mean spending more money. Say you've been saving money to buy a game. It sells online for almost $10 less than the store in town. Easy choice, right? But what if the game store in town is owned by a friend of your family who has two kids entering college and has always been generous to your school? It still might be an easy choice if you don't have that extra $10 to spend. Or you might decide to buy the game locally as a statement of your principles.

Another benefit to buying locally (besides supporting the local economy) is that the business owner may feel more accountable to you. If a small business disappoints you (maybe a favorite local restaurant switches to Styrofoam containers or maybe a local shop stopped carrying an eco-conscious brand you like), don't jump straight to a boycott (Action #108) or a Tweetstorm (Action #109), first write a letter, make a call, or stop by to ask them to reconsider what they're doing. The person-to-person interaction can be very effective.

111. Be upstanding

If you're anything like the rest of us, you're a good person who does many wonderful things and occasionally stuff you aren't so proud of (because, hey, we're all just humans trying to make our way in this world). Being your kindest, best self isn't always easy. It's a good thing you clearly aren't afraid of hard work!

Work hard to be upstanding. Be a real friend, avoid gossip or stirring the pot. Notice anyone vulnerable around you. Smile at them. Make room for them at your lunch table. If your friend says something that demeans or oversimplifies, practice speaking up (see Action #67). Be that person who doesn't smile at ugly jokes. Let your friends know that about you. Be that person who listens and thinks before reacting. Let your friends *trust* that about you.

If you've read this far, you're anxious to create a better world. Start right where you're standing, control what you can control, and walk confidently—intentionally—toward a better tomorrow.

CHAPTER NINE
Fundraising
Actions to Help You Raise Money

● ● ●

Dear Moneybags,

Wait, that's not you? Yeah, that's not me either. It's hard to be a less-than-flush advocate. Often you want to lend your passion and your time to an organization, but what they really need is your cash. And, be warned, if you have some money to kick in, more requests for money will start pouring in. Relentlessly!

The fact is, it all takes money. Amazing organizations need money, upstanders need funds, better candidates need financial support, and they'll all practically stare up at you with them big puppy-dog-eyes and pretty much beg. If you want to throw them a bone, this chapter will help you think of ways to raise a little money to do a little good. There are lots of ideas and some kibbles of sound advice. Give what you can give. Help how you can help. It's OK to say no.

Even if it's the cutest little organization you've ever seen, let me repeat: it's OK to say no. They may whimper a bit, but they'll understand.

Good advocate! Thanks for however you contribute!

Joanna

Part I: Get ready, get set, wait ... get organized first!

Before you and your terrific ideas set off to raise some moola, it's important that you do some prep work first. Sure it's not the glamorous part of the job—after all, no one is writing a news release about how she just spent two hours researching places to host a car wash!—but that doesn't mean that is not a vital part of the project. Put in the time to make a workable, concrete action plan for your fundraiser, and you are setting yourself up for success with your final result:

Step 1: Be sure to ask permission first.
It's pretty important to get your adult on board with any fundraising effort. Besides permission, ask if they'd be willing to help at the planning stage. Being open to hearing ideas and concerns speaks of your genuine commitment and will likely save you time and energy.

Step 2: Decide who you are raising money for and your (realistic) goal amount.

Know the who, what, and why. Who are you donating to? Is it legit? How much do you need? How did you come to that number? Think concretely. Rather than say you're raising money to help the homeless, call the shelter and ask to speak to the person in charge of donations. Ask them what specific needs they have, then plan accordingly. If the shelter says they could use washcloths, do your homework and come up with an exact figure. Set realistic goals.

Step 3: Plan an event appropriate to your time, money, and goals (see Part II). Evaluate how much time and money you *realistically* can devote to your project. Even if you plan on asking for help from friends or other well-meaning people, expect that things won't go perfectly according to plan, so be very realistic about what *you* can and cannot do, what *you* can and cannot afford.

Don't skip this step! Be sure that you're not spending so much on the fundraiser that you would be better off just donating that money somewhere instead. (Oh, how many, many, many, many times we have learned this lesson the hard way.) Until you get some real fundraising experience, it's wise to start small.

Step 4: Make a checklist of every single item you need.
List the big things like venue and number of volunteers and include the minutiae like plastic bags and staples. (Remember, it doesn't have to be Pinterest-worthy—maybe you don't need those

preprinted stickers to put on the cup at your lemonade stand and the oh-so-cute tablecloth.)

Step 5: Advertise your efforts! Ask your friends and family to help spread the word. Make fliers. Take photos. Tweet. Post. Send a news release (see Action #40).

Step 6: Take a mental walkthrough. Picture the event in your mind and take notes of what will go where, who will do what, and everything you need to have.

Step 7: Take a deep breath and enjoy the moment. Things won't always go as planned, that's a given, so don't panic. You're raising money for something you believe in, so take pride in your efforts!

May We Suggest ...

You may have noticed that certain organizations have come under fire lately. Those organizations need support, but with all the attention they're getting, money has been pouring in. Other, usually smaller, organizations might not be drawing as much attention and because they often count on the same donors for support, they might be overlooked. These smaller organizations might be working mighty hard to keep afloat. Look for causes that might not be first in everyone's mind.

Part II: The small, the medium, the big, the ginormo

Every person has their own reality. Maybe you have a lot of time and a little money, or maybe you have a lot of time and a decent amount of money, or maybe you're short on both. There are fundraising options that are realistic for each and every one of you—it's just a matter of finding the right fit. When your activism has reached the point where you need the money, go through this section to see what's a good fit for you and your fundraising and time needs.

112. Asking for help

If they have the means, an adult in your life may be delighted to support your activism—sometimes that support is financial, but sometimes it is emotional. If you know someone has money enough to do so, it is perfectly appropriate to ask them if they'd like to contribute to your efforts.

Take the time to sit down and write a well-crafted letter or email explaining what you're doing, how much you think you'll need, and—most important—what you hope to accomplish. Be sure to include a line that this person should feel no pressure to help you—that even an encouraging email or letter back would be a wonderful donation. No matter the contribution, don't forget the thank you card!

113. Every little bit helps

Good ole grandpappy used to say that if you watch your pennies, the dollars will follow—meaning, every little cent adds up. Yes, all the big groups and bigwigs and wannabe big players spend all sorts of time raising big, big money. But that's not the only way to fundraise. Crowdfunding sites have shown how effective it is to raise lots of money through lots of small donations. Here are a couple of ideas to raise smaller amounts through smallish time commitments:

- *Got change?* Collect loose change from friends, family, and neighbors (be sure to make it known what you're raising money for). You could also ask local businesses if you can leave a jar on their counter (be sure to go back once a week and collect).
- *Take a guess!* Going to be around a large group of family or friends soon? Let people know what you're doing these days and raise money, too. Fill a jar with jelly beans or buttons (or maybe Trump-induced tears?). Ask people to guess how many objects are in the jar: $1 per guess. (Is it hokey? Soooo hokey. But you probably will raise some money for what you care about as well as raise awareness. Hokey isn't so bad!) Use your elevator pitch (see Action #33) to tell people why you're raising money. (It's always these writers' best advice to pick the least controversial—least political— cause when trying to raise money from your own extended family. Just something to think about.)

114. Medium can be just right, too

Sometimes you have a little more time to commit to fundraise but that doesn't mean that you want to plunge yourself into something heart, soul, and wallet. This is when the medium fundraising is just right, to paraphrase our friend Goldilocks. Here are a couple ways to raise slightly bigger amounts of money with just a bit more effort:

- Make postcards to sell.
- Have a good old-fashioned lemonade stand.
- Host a bake sale.
- Do odd jobs for a purpose. (Walk dogs, rake leaves, mow lawns, run errands … all in the name of good.)

115. And every big bit helps, too

These are great actions to do with a group because they allow you to break up the workload into smaller bits for everyone. (But that's not to say that you can't also accomplish them on your own, too.) Here are a few bigly tasks to consider:

- Channel your inner Caine (cainesarcade.com), and host a cardboard arcade.
- Organize a neighborhood or virtual garage sale.
- Have a car wash.
- Hold a craft and art sale in person or sell online.

116. Go huge-ginormous-gigando

Ready to take a massive bite of the fundraising pie? These are the ideas that are best for groups. You might work with a service group; your church, synagogue, or mosque; or just the friends you hang out with. Divide the tasks and meet regularly to keep everyone on schedule.

- Have a danceathon.
- Host a local battle of the bands.
- Plan an open-mic night, poetry slam, or talent show (or a no-talent show?!).
- Hold a fun walk or run.

117. It's not always about the money, money, money...

Money isn't the only fundraising option. Have a drive instead where you collect items to pass on to an organization (*please* be sure to ask first what it is that they actually want and need). For example, you could collect canned goods for the local food pantry (if that's what they request), razors for a homeless shelter, books for a domestic violence shelter, backpacks for foster children, toiletries for undocumented immigrants at detainment centers, towels and bed linens for refugees, and so on. An important note: find a good-quality nonprofit to work with and—again—check with a worker there first to see what item would be most helpful.

118. Quiet gestures

Not every donation needs planning or fanfare. Small, quiet gestures can make a huge impact on our collective well-being. Consider baking a batch of cookies for the LGBTQ theater company in town, the attorneys staying vigilant at the airport, or the Muslim family down the road.

119. The worldwide wonders of virtual giving

Philanthropy has evolved with this generation's creativity, compassion, and understanding of the big ole Internet machine and how to best make use of its magical powers. Besides a virtual presence and one-click giving for almost every charity or organization on the planet, microloans and crowdsourcing have completely changed the giving model. There are lots of wonderful choices out there in the digital world. Here are a few of our favorites:

- Dosomething.org (www.dosomething.org) calls itself a global movement for good. The huge organization encourages young people to creatively engage for social change on and offline.
- Kiva (www.kiva.org) boasts creating over a billion dollars in change! Donate small loans to diverse borrowers all over the world. When loans are repaid, you can choose to take your money back or lend it to another borrower.
- The good people at YouCaring (www.youcaring.com) specialize in compassionate crowdsourcing. (Awesome, right?!) They offer a free platform to crowdsource medical, personal, and charitable causes.

CHAPTER TEN

Stay Inspired

Actions to Keep Yourself Motivated

● ● ●

"Compassion must be translated into action."

—NATASHA MAYERS,

ARTIST, EDUCATOR, AND ACTIVIST

Dear Fellow Fighter for Good,

This is it: our last chapter together. I hope that what the many activities in this book have taught you is that there are not only a lot of beautiful things in this country to fight for but that there are many, many ways to fight for them. But ... all of that fighting sounds a little exhausting, no?

Um, yeah, it sure as hell can be exhausting. And frustrating. And infuriating. This chapter is designed for *those* days, the ones when the fight starts to sound overwhelming. When you start feeling that way: *Don't. Give. Up.* This fight is not bigger than you—it may just feel that way at this particular second.

Instead, hit your pause button. Take a breath. Take four. Picture the world you are fighting for and remind yourself that you are in this not for the easy haul but for the long haul. Then give yourself a day or two, and turn to one (or more!) of the activities in this chapter to help refresh you and re-inspire until you are ready to *Wake, Rise, Resist* once more.

Love,
Kerri

120. Embrace your youthful thinking

You may have noticed that you don't think about things like adults do, at least not entirely. Please know that this is a gift. Some adults may try to dismiss it: they may call you naive or they may tell you that you don't understand the world. Don't listen to them. What this political world needs is more optimism and more out-of-the-box thinking. Always remember: #iamthefuture

The fact is, you're the present, too. *This* is your time to go bravely ahead with your own youthful understanding of the world and what is possible within it. *Now* is when you are needed. Get involved today: the future will be brighter for it!

121. Practice your pep talk

Sometimes the most powerful way to lift ourselves up is to help someone else feel better. This can be a scary time—an exceptional time, a tumultuous time; we all need the occasional reminder that we are not alone in the fight. In his final media conference, Barack Obama said, "I believe in this country. I believe in the American people. I think we're going to be okay." For this action, you're going to channel your inner Obama and reach out to remind someone else that everything is going to be okay. Call, text, or email another activist a pep talk to help lift her spirits and renew her energy to continue the fight for another day. (Are you the one who needs a pep talk? Call a like-minded friend or family member to boost you up. Or if that's not an option, go to YouTube and gorge on some videos of inspiring political speeches. See Action #122.)

122. Relight your fire

It is disheartening to think about where the country is and what its political power looks like right now. When you feel your flame of activism and positivity starting to flicker, don't forget that we have had some amazing presidents and leaders who have done important work, who have taken courageous stands, who have agonized on our behalf. We've had presidents who have inspired millions of people worldwide. Go on YouTube to fire yourself back up by watching some speeches from these kinds of leaders: check out JFK's inauguration speech, MLK's "I Have a Dream" speech,

Barack Obama's 2004 keynote DNC address, and Obama's "More Perfect Union" speech on race.

Also don't miss Michelle Obama's 2016 DNC speech, which can offer us all some words to continue to live by. Sure, she was talking about the election, but the advice continues to inspire: "We cannot sit back and hope that everything works out for the best," she said. "We cannot afford to be tired or frustrated or cynical." We still cannot afford this, young activist. Go forward with conviction and positivity and be fired up. #iamthefuture

123. Practice gratitude

Look around you. Despite the real issues facing your world, scan your environment for something you like, something you're grateful for. You can feel gratitude for the huge things like loving and supportive people but don't forget to look for the little things—the splash of sprinkles on the donut you ate this morning, the warmth of your bed, the cheery square of yellow sunlight on the kitchen floor. Make seeing the world with grateful eyes your habit. Such practices are thought to reduce pain, anger, and fear while making people feel happier, more connected, and more accepting. You may want to start a gratitude journal or ask a friend or parent to practice gratitude with you via text or around the table. You will be shocked at how much a consistent practice of gratitude will improve your mood.

May We Suggest ...

A fun way to bring the whole family into the practice of gratitude is to start a Crappy/Happy routine. Pick a time when you are all most likely to be together (depending on your family's schedule, it could be daily like the drive to an activity or weekly like Saturday breakfast). Each person should talk about something "crappy" that happened to them recently (bad news or something just kind of crummy) and then follow up with something "happy" (good news or just something kinda nice you recently noticed.)

124. Send out vibes

If you like how gratitude feels, take it a step further and try meditation. Loving-kindness meditation, for example, is the act of silently sending out kindness vibes to the world. Sound hokey? Totally! But it works. Memorize this mantra: "May you be happy. May you be well. May you be safe. May you be peaceful and at ease." Now for the hokey part: Silently say the mantra a few times a day; maybe when you're brushing your teeth or walking through the grocery store. Say it for yourself, and send it toward people you love and even people you don't. Loving-kindness meditation is like exercise. It builds your compassion muscles! It also comforts and calms you. Try it. (Find that you like meditating? Check out an app such as Calm to practice more meditations.)

May We Suggest ...

Want more of that sort of comfort and calm? Try yoga! Yoga has a way of both making you focus more on yourself and simultaneously helping you feel a connection to all things. You don't need a fancy studio membership to do it. Just check out the beginner yoga videos on YouTube until you find someone you like. The website Yome: Your Home for Yoga (yogameditationhome.com) also has good options.

125. You lead; we'll follow

If you've read this far, it's a good time to thank you for your commitment and your compassion. We hope to have given you some inspiration and some ideas, but, really, we're counting on *you*. You and your peers are the innovators, the creative thinkers, and the problem-solvers. Today we all may be reacting, but tomorrow it's your lead. And you're already well on your way. Study up on the many amazing organizations that will help you build your leadership skills, and see if any are active in your area. If not, write to them and ask them to refer you to a similar organization closer to home. Here are some ideas to get you started on your search:

- 4-H: 4-h.org
- Boys and Girls Clubs of America: www.bgca.org
- Girl Scouts: www.girlscouts.org

- Global Kids: www.globalkids.org
- Key Club International: www.keyclub.org
- Kiwanis K-Kids: kiwaniskids.org

126. Walk the walk

One of the most powerful gifts that any one person can give the world is to serve as an example for others. Sometimes the best way to feel good is by knowing that you are doing your part to make a difference. So continue to stand strong in your beliefs, and continue to live the way *you* believe to be right—no matter what the world around you seems to be saying. So if you want to be a warrior for the environment, *live* like a warrior for the environment. (Maybe walk or bike to the pool or to the store rather than drive, and drink water when you're thirsty rather than having a bottled beverage that will add to the waste stream.) Or if you believe that the United States' diversity makes us stronger, then celebrate that diversity. The next time you're out, sit next to the kid that looks different from you. Strike up a conversation. And then you, young activist, are walking the walk—not just talking the talk.

Go the Extra Step

Keep a journal or chart of all of your activism to show yourself how much you have done to try to make a difference. In this marathon of improving where our country is headed, the path can feel long: your record of activism will help you see how far you have come and how much you have contributed.

127. Take care!

Activism might feel like a long, slow slog at times. It can take a toll on you emotionally and even physically. Staying engaged in the issues you care about can feel lonely and/or exhausting—especially when it's hard to see all of the small changes you are slowly bringing about. Be sure to also give yourself what you need to keep on resisting: unplug from time to time, blow off steam talking to like-minded friends about your frustrations, give yourself a day or two of vacation from thinking about it. (But don't forget what a privilege it is to *not have* to think about something all the time.). And—most important—if you feel really sad or worried, talk to someone at school or at home who can help. But whatever you do, DO NOT GIVE UP. We are in for the long haul here. Expect some mental exhaustion, expect some frustration, and expect some defeats. Do not let any of those hold you back from fighting for the world that we all know we need.

128. Find your inspiration

We, Joanna and Kerri, have spent our almost 20 years of friendship inspiring each other and challenging each other and educating each other and growing together. What we wish for *you* now is that you will find a friend who also pushes you to always be and think and act as your best self (and who understands when you're just not feeling up to being your best self that particular day).

Changing the world isn't a solo project. You're gonna need some allies. Find your Joanna. Find your Kerri. Find someone who makes you a better person and who pushes you to be involved and who listens to your ranting when the political landscape gets frustrating. Find someone who helps you do crazy things like bike more than 500 miles to benefit AIDS charities (true story!). Find the friend who will say, "Hey, let's write a book of actions for young progressives!" Find someone who pushes you to be your best you and that will be the best motivation of all for staying positive and staying true to your values. Good luck!

HOW TO FIND WHAT YOU'RE LOOKING FOR
IN THIS BOOK

● ● ●

Dear Reader,

Well, this seems like as good of a place as any to admit to you that we don't really know what we're doing. (Is that OK to say to you now that you've read our book? Let's say yes.) You see, while we are both writers and editors, we've never really written a book-book before—at least not one that comes straight from our hearts (and straight from our quietly angsty places).

We think we taught ourselves pretty well and are super-proud of this effort. But here is where the jig will be up: We're not really indexers. So we are going to kinda, sorta index for you here to help you find what you're looking for in our book— but we are doing that out of pure love for you, dear reader, and not from any special knowledge of how to index well or properly. All of which is to say that we probably missed a lot of stuff in this index. All we can say to that is: love us for our passion and creativity, not for our organization skills.

Yours imperfectly but passionately,

Joanna and Kerri

THE PASSION INDEX

• • •

Below is a list of several of the issues that the modern progressive movement stands for (or against). Look at it, learn it, love it (and then turn to the listed action number and live it). Action numbers listed here are items where these topics are specifically mentioned—but use any of the actions in the book toward what you are passionate about!

Disability Rights #11, #31

Economic Activism #77, #92, #93, #105, #106, #107, #108, #110, Chapter 9

Economic Justice #63, #77

Environment and Climate Change #31, #69, #78, #79, #107

Fair and Impartial Policing #31, #73

Free Speech and Media #35, #40, #43, #80

Gun Violence #34c, #76

Health Care #11, #72, #75

Immigration and Refugees Justice #13, #21, #28, #31, #35, #68

Islamophobia #13, #16, #21, #31, #27, #68

LGBTQ+ Equality #14, #31, #74

Military and Veteran Affairs #24, #82
Money in Politics #32, #71, #77
Racial Justice and Social Justice #13, #31, #73
Voting #11, #71, #81, #94
Women's Issues and Reproductive Justice #11, #31, #60, #61, #76
Workers' Rights and Consumer Protections #77

Activities for Certain Moods

Feel like writing?
#23, #35, #40, #44, #47, #66,

Feel like being artsy?
#9, #37, #44, #87, #93, #94

Feel like learning about something new?
#6, #7, #19, #20, #29, #61, #63, #71, #72, #77, #80, #107, #124

Feel like hanging out with friends?
#36, #37, #44, #66, #79, #85, #88, #91, #95 #98, #99, #109, Chapter 9

Feel like making your voice heard?
#34a, #34b, #35, #36, #37, #40, #44, #45, #80, #83, #90, #109

Feel like using social media?

#31, #36, #37, #84, #105, #109

Feeling down and need an instant pop of accomplishment?

#7, #32, #33, #39, #45, Chapter 6, #96, #105, #107, #118, #119, #123

Feel like doing good with your family?

#8, #9, #42, #51, #78, #82, #83, #88, #91, #96, #103, #117, #118, #123

Trying to understand privilege?

#11, #25, #57, #58, #59, #60, #61, #65, #73

ACKNOWLEDGEMENTS

• • •

We are unique beasts, but comfort is trusting that others understand. First, I want to thank everyone who openly, boldly resists. I am thrilled to be on your side.

For all my politically engaged role models—from the stories of the *palia Mousakata* through the NMSU Women's Studies Department, to the rigorous Facebook groups, all the way to Progressives for Change Elmhurst—THANK YOU.

To my dad, who taught me to connect the dots so that I would feel compelled to engage; to my mom who fostered my emotional I.Q. so that I could participate in authentic relationships; to Harriet and Ronald for the perspective and the wine; to Virginia; to all my family, close and extended; to Lesvia and Sierra; to each of the friends of my lifetime—the girlfriends who shared vulnerabilities and abundant support—THANK YOU. It has been my absolute honor. Especially you, Ker.

And to Thomas—my brilliant, steadfast husband—for your patient support and comic relief and for exceeding my every possible dream of a partner by every possible measure. I really do.

–Joanna

I must start with thanks for my family, who invested in me a love of learning, a passion for kindness, and a penchant for sarcasm. Dad, thanks for always asking me when I was going to finally write that book. Mom, thanks for being my shoulder to cry on and my model of giving. For Kim and Kandi, thank you for not accidentally killing me during those bike rides when I was a baby and thank you for always, *always* being there when I need you. I won the family lottery. (And, of course, for Grandma: a passionate activist before I even understood what the hell that was.)

To Jo, my Valentine, who made this all possible. I'm glad I wrote you for a snack intervention all of those years ago. I had a good eye!

Also, thank you to the Flaming D's and the Gamers for being wonderful friends who constantly amaze me with their equal capacities for hugely entertaining smart-ass-ery and awesomely inspiring compassion. Thanks, too, to the many who have inspired me since the election—especially those in Progressives for Change: you all have been a lifesaver.

And thank you to the faraway friends who put up with months of haphazardly answered texts during the course of writing this book. I miss you all!

To my fierce, caring, inspiring, feminist girls Libby and Emma, I thank you for reminding me daily of the good in the world. (But sorry, ladies: Hoppy is still my favorite child.)

And to Martin, who is (almost) always able to make me laugh. I think I'll keep him.

–Kerri

To our sensitivity editor, Jessica Davis, who made this book about a trillion times better and whose depth of knowledge and perfect feedback were the inspiring nudge forward just when we needed it. Jessica, we (and the world) are lucky to have you and your passion. Find her work at medium.com/@jessicadavis_96034 or write her at Jessd0806@gmail.com.

–Joanna and Kerri

ABOUT THE AUTHORS

• • •

Joanna Spathis is a writer, activist, volunteer, and unflinching Liberal. She lives with her husband and three kids just outside of Chicago ... and across the street from Kerri.

Kerri Kennedy is a writer, editor, former high school teacher, and proud card-carrying ACLU member. She is also an excellent raider of Joanna's perfectly nearby and perfectly stocked pantry.

CPSIA information can be obtained
at www.ICGtesting.com
Printed in the USA
LVOW13s1613150318
569991LV00010B/649/P